To Beth, Ken, and Joe Spina, as well as all the smaller, fuzzier Spinas that have joined us along the way

The Unlucky Investor's Guide to Options Trading

Julia Spina

Coauthored by Anton Kulikov

Foreword by Tom Sosnoff

WILEY

Published by John Wiley & Sons, Inc., Hoboken, New Jersey.
Published simultaneously in Canada.

For general information on our other products and services or for technical support, please contact our Customer Care Department within the United States at (800) 762-2974, outside the United States at (317) 572-3993 or fax (317) 572-4002.

Wiley also publishes its books in a variety of electronic formats. Some content that appears in print may not be available in electronic formats. For more information about Wiley products, visit our web site at www.wiley.com.

Library of Congress Cataloging-in-Publication Data is Available:

ISBN: 9781394278060 (Paperback)
ISBN: 9781119882671 (ePDF)
ISBN: 9781119882664 (ePub)

Cover Design and Image: © Cassie Scroggins
SKY10082657_082324

The ace-ace-nine is an inside joke at tastytrade and quite possibly the most annoying way to lose a hand of blackjack. Blackjack, for those unfamiliar with gambling, is a game between a dealer and player where the objective is to get closest to 21 without exceeding it. Face cards are worth 10 and aces are worth either 1 or 11. Imagine being at a blackjack table sitting pretty with 20, and the dealer is showing an ace. They confirm they don't have blackjack, turn over their second card and show another ace. The round is basically won and done because the dealer has a terrible hand, totaling 2 or 12, against your 20. The dealer draws their third card and reveals a nine, and by the time you've done the math, the house has already taken your chips.

Contents

Foreword

I've come a long way from my knuckle-dragging pit trading days of the 1980s and 1990s. I take the wrapper *off* hot dogs when I eat them now, and I have also learned a few things about investing after 20 years of meeting people all over the country and teaching them how to trade. One crazy takeaway: Unlucky investors usually make the best traders. Why? Because anyone can get lucky and profit from a random investment, but in the small world of successful traders, the common denominator is quantitative skill. Another crazy takeaway: Anyone can learn these skills with access to the right information.

Way back when TD Ameritrade bought thinkorswim in 2009, I negotiated with every bit of leverage I had to personally keep the domain name, tastytrade.com. I had purchased the web address for $9.95 years earlier through GoDaddy, and I was convinced, just as I was with thinkorswim, that the name tastytrade would work. I have no idea why I loved tastytrade.com, but sometimes hunches just seem to work out. tastytrade's raison d'être was to fill the void in the financial media and offer up an untested, goodwill model built around raw, math-based content. We've spent the last 10 years obsessively building client engagement by introducing complex financial strategies to retail investors. We still answer questions 24 hours a day and teach lessons from what we learned as market makers and software entrepreneurs: all for free. We truly are the guest who won't leave, but we believe that nonstop client engagement is core to motivating traders.

I have so many special memories from the last two decades, but one of my favorites was a strange trading story from an early 2001 trip to the desert. It was the first time we did a live trading show in Las Vegas, and a big trader at the event asked me how long it would take to get a fill on a large order using our platform. When I asked for his order, the client told me he wanted 10,000 spreads. This was before electronic spread executions existed, and I figured he was bullshitting me. But, as a show of good faith (and because I didn't want to back down), I told him we'd fill the order within one second. The client was convinced it wasn't going to happen, so I was pretty pleased when I told him, hand signal and all, that his order was filled in less than a second and the price improved by a nickel. We made asses of ourselves, but this is how it all began. Over the years, we continued to form unbreakable relationships with hundreds of thousands of amazing friends, traders, and investors. We gambled together, ate dinner together, had drinks at the bar, laughed when we made money, and cried when we lost money. We told jokes, embarrassed ourselves, humbled each other, and tortured our friends. We focused on building those relationships not only because it was a blast but because we also really saw how it motivated people to learn how to trade and participate in the market. It was key to the success of thinkorswim, and it inspired the founding of tastytrade.

When we started tastytrade, our proving ground was an old hip-hop studio in downtown Chicago. It was a third-floor walk-up with a piano as the receptionist's desk and a drum set in the middle of the living room. Old album covers and broken musical instruments were everywhere, yet the energy was undeniable. Our research team consisted of a Guitar Hero champion in a hot dog suit, a few interns, and an ex-market maker. Our mentor was a sports shock jock whose claim to fame was having sex on the 50-yard line at Soldier Field, and to top it all off, we had hired a bunch of random comedians from Chicago's famed Second City. Thank God we knew how to trade because we had no clue how to do media. Even worse, I will never forget the day we decided to do HD quality video. I thought, "No way is that what I look like." That's why tastytrade is so awesome because we figured out a totally new model of financial media when the odds were against us.

Lucky investors never figure things out because they never have to: They simply follow the herd and hope for the best. We refused to follow traditional financial media down the path of self-promotion and financial irrelevance. We found smart people, fed them cheap lunches, made them work crazy hours, gave them free snacks, and mostly let them do their own thing. The result? We changed the world of strategic investing.

We knew early on that a book about options trading would add a new layer to our model of engagement and be a powerful tool for creating financial content. Eighteen years ago, I locked myself in our old conference room with one of our cofounders, and we tried to write a book. We hired a professional writer, cleared our schedules, and made the book a priority. Three days later and one and half pages in, we fired the writer and quit the book project to protect our friendship and the future of our firm. Fast forward to early 2021, and I was again bitten by the book bug, but this time, I knew I wasn't up to the task. I asked, as nicely as I am capable of, for two of our young, smart researchers to help. I said, "It's all yours." Julia and Anton accepted the challenge, and they totally nailed it. I truly believe this is the most logical, informative, and comprehensive book on strategic options trading ever compiled. Unlucky investors can rejoice. No book will ever be a one-size-fits-all holy grail for options trading, but *The Unlucky Investor's Guide to Options Trading* is the closest thing we have.

Tom Sosnoff

Preface

If the conditions are just right, extraordinary things happen when many individual pieces come together: Water molecules organize and form snowflakes; Cells arrange and create organs; Jet streams combine and cause tornadoes; Grains of sand rally and produce avalanches; Investors panic sell and induce financial crashes. Complex systems are composed of many interacting parts, and *emergence* occurs when these parts organize to create collective phenomena that no one part is capable of creating alone. Complex systems can be found in nearly every discipline, and the mathematics describing emergent properties is not only fascinating but indicates fundamental similarities between seemingly unrelated complex systems. The extinction of a species of fly due to an invasive species of frog has really nothing to do with financial markets, yet the dynamics of the fly population undergoing ecological collapse look nearly indistinguishable from that of a stock undergoing economic collapse. Many physicists gravitate toward finance because physical systems and financial systems can be analyzed with similar theoretical, statistical, and computational tools. It was my interest in those mathematical connections that drew me to finance initially. However, after placing my first trade at the start of the

2020 crash, I quickly learned the importance of financial intuition as well, particularly when trading options.

A trader's intuition comes from experience, but a trader can more efficiently build that intuition by supplementing market engagement with some basic trading philosophies. Many of the papers, books, and blogs I read as a new options trader offered detailed coverage of options theory and its mathematics, but I never encountered a resource that explicitly laid out the most essential elements of practical strategy development. Without a system of core trading principles, applying financial theory, interpreting and analyzing data, and cultivating any sense of market intuition was challenging. However, once a foundation of options trading fundamentals was in place, overcoming the options learning curve became a considerably more manageable process. In my personal case, this foundation developed from conversations with my coworkers at tastytrade (most of which were debates with Anton Kulikov), watching options markets regularly, using options data and theory to build actionable strategies, and a lot of trial and error. My goal in writing this book is to help new traders build their own intuitions more effectively by breaking down the philosophies that formed the basis for my own, beginning with a bit of math and market theory and building from there. Nothing substitutes for experience, and investors' first options trade will likely teach them more than any book. However, it's my hope this framework that Anton and I organized will allow new traders to enter the options market with confidence and gain meaningful value from their first trading experiences, in both the monetary and educational senses.

Julia Spina

Acknowledgments

This world is full of uncertainties, but I'm fairly certain this project would have ended in disaster without the hard work of some very talented people. First and foremost, this book would not have been possible without Tom Sosnoff. Tom originally proposed the project and has wholeheartedly supported my work and opinions throughout this entire process. He is a great boss and never short of awesome restaurant recommendations. The primary editor, Erika Cohen, has not only been highly competent but also wonderful to work with. Involved since the beginning, she played a huge role organizing our ideas, and her insights greatly enhanced the readability and accessibility of the material. I wish only the best for her and her family. The technical editor, Jacob Perlman, has also been crucial in this book's development. His work at tastytrade years ago laid the groundwork for many of the ideas presented in this book, and it continues to inspire retail traders to this day. His mathematical expertise has improved the accuracy and presentation of the technical concepts covered, and I cannot speak more highly of his abilities.

On the publishing front, Jeff Joseph has been instrumental in transforming our series of drafts into a proper book. He has been immensely helpful in organizing the logistics of the publication process, offering creative advice, and establishing our relationship with Wiley. This book would not have been possible without everyone on the highly skilled editorial team at Wiley, who have all put an exceptional amount of effort into this book. Many people have contributed to the project throughout this process, but those I have collaborated with most closely include Bill Falloon, Purvi Patel, Manikandan Kuppan, Susan Cerra, and Samantha Wu. I'd also like to acknowledge the artistic contributions of Cassie Scroggins, who did a fantastic job designing the cover.

I am also grateful for the content advice from Thomas Preston, who never shied away from my many phone calls, and the writing advice from Vonetta Logan. It should be noted that everyone at tastytrade, especially the research team, has directly or indirectly had a hand in making this book possible. The ideas presented in this book were not built from scratch but rather the successes and failures of all the talented content creators at tastytrade over many years of collaboration.

Julia Spina

About the Authors

Julia Spina is member of the research team and podcast co-host at tastytrade where she works as a financial educator and options strategist. Drawing from her background in physics and experience with signal processing and data analysis, Julia introduces viewers to topics in quantitative finance and their applications in options strategy development. Prior to transitioning into finance, Julia worked as a regenerative medicine research scientist before attending the University of Illinois at Urbana-Champaign in 2015. At the University of Illinois, she earned bachelor's degrees in engineering physics (2017) and applied mathematics (2017) and a master's in physics (2018). Her research focus throughout her graduate and undergraduate studies was experimental quantum optics, and her primary projects included investigating the effects of measurement in optical quantum systems and using single-photon sources to determine the lower limits of human vision and perception.

Anton Kulikov is a member of the research team and podcast co-host at tastytrade and a columnist for the financial lifestyle magazine, *Luckbox*. With a background in finance, data science, and education, he has spent the last four years developing innovative strategies for the retail options market and educating traders in fundamental economic theory on the show. Anton attended the University of Illinois at Urbana-Champaign where he earned bachelor's degrees in finance (2018) and economics (2018) and worked at the Margolis Market Information Lab. During his time at the University of Illinois, Anton developed coursework on derivatives and capital markets, and taught classes and workshops on financial software at the Gies College of Business.

Tom Sosnoff is an online brokerage innovator, financial educator, and the founder and co-CEO of tastytrade. Tom is a serial entrepreneur who cofounded thinkorswim in 1999, tastytrade in 2011, tastyworks in 2017, helped to launch the award-winning *Luckbox* magazine in 2019, and in 2020 created the first new futures exchange in 20 years, The Small Exchange. Leveraging more than 20 years of experience as a CBOE market maker, Tom is driven by the passion to educate self-directed investors. After his years on the trading floor, he saw the need to build and design superior software platforms and brokerage firms that specialized in complex financial strategies. His efforts ultimately changed the way options and futures are traded and how digital financial media is produced and consumed. Currently, Tom hosts *tastytrade LIVE* and continues to drive innovation and know-how for the do-it-yourself investor. Tom has been named to *Techweek*'s Tech 100 list, *Crain's Chicago Business*'s Tech 50, and has spoken at more than 500 events across the globe. Tom received the Ernst & Young Entrepreneur of the Year Award and has been featured by prominent publications such as the *The Wall Street Journal, Investor's Business Daily, Chicago Tribune, Crain's Chicago Business, Traders Magazine,* and *Barron's.*

Introduction: Why Trade Options?

*T**he house always wins.** This cautionary quote is certainly true, but it does not tell the entire story. From table limits to payout odds, every game in a casino is designed to give the house a statistical edge. The casino may take large, infrequent losses at the slot machines or small, frequent losses at the blackjack table, but as long as patrons play long enough, the house will inevitably turn a profit. Casinos have long relied on this principle as the foundation of their business model: People can either bet *against* the house and hope that luck lands in their favor or *be* the house and have probability on their side.

Unlike casinos, where the odds are fixed against the players, liquid financial markets offer a dynamic, level playing field with more room to strategize. However, similar to casinos, a successful trader does not rely on luck. Rather, traders' long-term success depends on their ability to obtain a consistent, statistical edge from the tools, strategies, and information available to them. Today's markets are becoming increasingly accessible to the average person, as online and commission-free trading have basically become industry standards. Investors have access to an almost unlimited selection of strategies, and options play an interesting role in this development. An option is a type of financial contract that gives the holder the right to buy or sell an asset on or before some future date, a concept that will be explained more in the following chapter. Options have tunable risk-reward profiles, allowing traders to reliably select the probability of profit, max loss, and max profit of a position and potentially profit in any type of market (bullish, bearish, or neutral). These highly versatile instruments can be used to hedge risk and diversify a portfolio, *or* options can be structured to give more risk-tolerant traders a probabilistic edge.

In addition to being customizable according to specific risk-reward preferences, options are also tradable with accounts of nearly any size because they are *leveraged* instruments. In the world of options, leverage refers to the ability to gain or lose more than the initial investment of a trade. An investor may pay $100 for an option and make $200 by the end of the trade, or an investor may make $100 by selling an option and lose $200 by the end of the trade. Leverage may seem unappealing because of its association with risk, but it is not inherently dangerous. When *misused*, leverage can easily wreak financial havoc. However, when used responsibly, the capital efficiency of leverage is a powerful tool that enables traders to achieve the same risk-return exposure as a stock position with significantly less capital.

There is no free lunch in the market. A leveraged instrument that has a 70% chance of profiting must come with some trade-off of risk, risk which may even be undefined in some cases. This is why the core principle of sustainable options trading is risk management. Just as casinos control the size of jackpot payouts by limiting the maximum amount a player can bet, options traders must control their exposure to potential losses from leveraged positions by limiting position size. And just as casinos diversify risk across different games with different odds, strategy diversification is essential to the long-term success of an options portfolio.

Beyond the potential downside risk of options, other factors can make them unattractive to investors. Unlike equities, which are passive instruments, options require a more active trading approach due to their volatile nature and time sensitivity. Depending on the choice of strategies, options portfolios should be monitored anywhere from daily to once every two weeks. Options trading also has a fairly steep learning curve and requires a larger base of math knowledge compared to equities. Although the mathematics of options can easily become complicated and burdensome, for the type of options trading covered in this book, trading decisions can often be made with a selection of indicators and intuitive, back-of-the-envelope calculations.

The goal of this book is to educate traders to make personalized and informed decisions that best align with their unique profit goals and risk tolerances. Using statistics and historical backtests, this book contextualizes the downside risk of options, explores the strategic capacity of these contracts, and emphasizes the key risk management techniques in building a resilient options portfolio. To introduce these concepts in a straightforward way, this book begins with discussion of the math and finance basics of quantitative options trading (Chapter 1), followed by an intuitive explanation of implied volatility (Chapter 2) and trading short premium (Chapter 3). With these foundational concepts covered, the book then moves onto trading in practice, beginning with buying power reduction and option leverage (Chapter 4), followed by trade construction (Chapter 5) and trade management (Chapter 6). Chapter 7 covers essential topics in portfolio management, and Chapter 8 covers supplementary topics in advanced portfolio management. Chapter 9 provides a brief commentary on atypical trades (Binary Events). The book concludes with a final chapter of key takeaways (Chapter 10) and an appendix of mathematical topics.

Chapter 1

Math and Finance Preliminaries

The purpose of this book is to provide a *qualitative* framework for options investing based on a *quantitative* analysis of financial data and theory. Mathematics plays a crucial role when developing this framework, but it is predominantly a means to an end. This chapter therefore includes a brief overview of the prerequisite math and financial concepts required to understand this book. Because this isn't in-depth coverage of the following topics, we encourage you to explore the supplemental texts listed in the references section for those mathematically inclined. Formulae and their descriptions are included in several sections for reference, but they are not necessary to follow the remainder of the book.

Stocks, Exchange-Traded Funds, and Options

From swaptions to non-fungible tokens (NFTs), new instruments and opportunities frequently emerge as markets evolve. By the time this book reaches the shelf, the financial landscape and the instruments occupying it may be very different from when it was written. Rather than focus on a wide range of instruments, this book discusses fundamental trading concepts using a small selection of asset classes (stocks, exchange-traded funds, and options) to formulate examples.

A share of *stock* is a security that represents a fraction of ownership of a corporation. Stock shares are normally issued by the corporation as a source of funding, and these instruments are usually publicly traded on stock exchanges, such as the New York Stock Exchange (NYSE) and the Nasdaq. Shareholders are entitled to a fraction of the company's assets and profits based on the proportion of shares they own relative to the number of outstanding shares.

An *exchange-traded fund (ETF)* is a basket of securities, such as stocks, bonds, or commodities. Like stocks, shares of ETFs are traded publicly on stock exchanges. Similar to mutual funds, these instruments represent a fraction of ownership of a diversified portfolio that is usually managed professionally. These assets track aspects of the market such as an index, sector, industry, or commodity. For example, SPDR S&P 500 (SPY) is a market index ETF tracking the S&P 500, Energy Select Sector SPDR Fund (XLE) is a sector ETF tracking the energy sector, and SPDR Gold Trust (GLD) is a commodity ETF tracking gold. ETFs are typically much cheaper to trade than the individual assets in an ETF portfolio and are inherently diversified. For instance, a share of stock for an energy company is subject to company-specific risk factors, while a share of an energy ETF is diversified over several energy companies.

When assessing the price dynamics of a stock or ETF and comparing the dynamics of different assets, it is common to convert price information into returns. The return of a stock is the amount the stock price increased or decreased as a proportion of its value rather than a dollar amount. Returns can be scaled over any time frame (daily, monthly, annual), with calculations typically calling for daily returns. The two most common types of returns are simple returns, represented as a percentage and calculated using Equation (1.1), and log returns, calculated using Equation (1.2). The logarithm's mathematical definition and properties are covered in the appendix for those interested, but that information is not necessary to know to follow the remainder of the book.

$$\text{Simple Returns} = R_t = \frac{S_t - S_{t-1}}{S_{t-1}} \tag{1.1}$$

$$\text{Log Returns} = R_t = \ln\left(\frac{S_t}{S_{t-1}}\right) \qquad (1.2)$$

where S_t is the price of the asset on day t and S_{t-1} is the price of the asset the prior day. For example, an asset priced at \$100 on day 1 and \$101 on day 2 has a simple daily return of 0.01 (1%) and a log return of 0.00995. Simple and log returns have different mathematical characteristics (e.g., log returns are time-additive), which impact more advanced quantitative analysis. However, these factors are not relevant for the purposes of this book because the difference between log returns and simple returns is fairly negligible when working on daily timescales. Simple daily returns are used for all returns calculations shown.

An *option* is a type of financial derivative, meaning its price is based on the value of an underlying asset. Options contracts are either traded on public exchanges (exchange-traded options) or traded privately with little regulatory oversight (over-the-counter [OTC] options). As OTC options are nonstandardized and usually inaccessible for retail investors, only exchange-traded options will be discussed in this book.

An option gives the holder the right (but not the obligation) to buy or sell some amount of an underlying asset, such as a stock or ETF, at a predetermined price on or before a future date. The two most common styles of options are American and European options. American options can be exercised at any point prior to expiration, and European options can only be exercised on the expiration date.[1] Because American options are generally more popular than European options and offer more flexibility, this book focuses on American options.

The most basic types of options are calls and puts. American *calls* give the holder the right to *buy* the underlying asset at a certain price within a given time frame, and American *puts* give the holder the right to *sell* the underlying asset. The contract parameters must be specified prior to opening the trade and are listed below:

- The underlying asset trading at the spot price, or the current per share price (S).
- The number of underlying shares. One option usually covers 100 shares of the underlying, known as a one lot.

---

[1] In liquid markets, which will be discussed in Chapter 5, American and European options are mathematically very similar.

- The price at which the underlying shares can be bought or sold prior to expiration. This price is called the strike price (K).
- The expiration date, after which the contract is worthless. The time between the present day and the expiration date is the contract's duration or days to expiration (DTE).

Note that the price of the option is commonly denoted as C for calls, P for puts, and V if the type of contract is not specified. Options traders may buy or sell these contracts, and the conditions for profitability differ depending on the choice of position. The purchaser of the contract pays the option premium (current market price of the option) to adopt the *long* side of the position. This is also known as a long premium trade. The seller of the contract receives the option premium to adopt the *short* side of the position, thus placing a short premium trade. The choice of strategy corresponds to the directional assumption of the trader. For calls and puts, the directional assumption is either bullish, assuming the underlying price will increase, or bearish, assuming the underlying price will decrease. The directional assumptions and scenarios for profitability for these contracts are summarized in the following table.

Table 1.1   The definitions, conditions for profitability, and directional assumptions for long/short calls/puts.

	Call	Put
	Purchase the right to buy an underlying asset (S) at the strike price (K) prior to the expiration date.	Purchase the right to sell an underlying asset (S) at the strike price (K) prior to the expiration date.
Long	Profits increase as the price of the underlying increases above the strike price ($S > K$).	Profits increase as the price of the underlying decreases below the strike price ($S < K$).
	Directional assumption: Bullish	Directional assumption: Bearish
	Sell the right to buy an underlying asset (S) at the strike price (K) prior to the expiration date.	Sell the right to sell an underlying asset (S) at the strike price (K) prior to the expiration date.
Short	Profits increase as the price of the underlying decreases below the strike price ($S < K$).	Profits increase as the price of the underlying increases above the strike price ($S > K$).
	Directional assumption: Bearish	Directional assumption: Bullish

The relationship between the strike price and the current price of the underlying determines the *moneyness* of the position. This is equivalently the *intrinsic value* of a position, or the value of the contract if it were exercised immediately. Contracts can be described as one of the following, noting that options cannot have negative intrinsic value:

- In-the-money (ITM): The contract would be profitable if it was exercised immediately and thus has intrinsic value.
- Out-of-the-money (OTM): The contract would result in a loss if it was exercised immediately and thus has no intrinsic value.
- At-the-money (ATM): The contract has a strike price equal to the price of the underlying and thus has no intrinsic value.

The intrinsic value of a position is based entirely on the type of position and the choice of strike price relative to the price of the underlying:

- Call options
  - Intrinsic Value = Either $S - K$ (stock price − strike price) or 0
  - ITM: $S > K$
  - OTM: $S < K$
  - ATM: $S = K$
- Put options
  - Intrinsic Value = Either $K - S$ or 0
  - ITM: $S < K$
  - OTM: $S > K$
  - ATM: $S = K$

For example, consider a 45 DTE put contract with a strike price of $100:

- Scenario 1 (ITM): The underlying price is $95. In this case, the intrinsic value of the put contract is $5 per share.
- Scenario 2 (OTM): The underlying price is $105. In this case, the put contract has no intrinsic value.
- Scenario 3 (ATM): The underlying price is $100. In this case, the put is also considered to have no intrinsic value.

The value of an option also depends on speculative factors, driven by supply and demand. The *extrinsic* value of the option is the difference between the current market price for the option and the intrinsic value of the option. Again, consider a 45 DTE put contract with a strike price of $100 on an underlying with a current price per share of $105. Suppose that, due to a period of recent market turbulence, investors are fearful the underlying price will crash within the next 45 days and create a demand for these OTM put contracts. The surge in demand inflates the price of the put contract to $10 per share. Therefore, because the put contract has no intrinsic value but has a market price of $10, the extrinsic value of the contract is $10 per share. If, instead, the price of the underlying is $95 and the price of the ITM put is still $10 per share, then the contract will have $5 in intrinsic value and $5 in extrinsic value.

The profitability of an option ultimately depends on both intrinsic and extrinsic factors, and it is calculated as the difference between the intrinsic value of an option and the cost of the contract. Mathematically, profit and loss (P/L) approximations for long calls and puts at exercise are given by the following equations:[2]

$$\text{Long call P/L} = max(0, S - K) - C \qquad (1.3)$$

$$\text{Long put P/L} = max(0, K - S) - P \qquad (1.4)$$

where the max function simply outputs the larger of the two values. For instance, $max(0, 1)$ equals 1 while $max(0, -1)$ equals 0. The P/Ls for the corresponding short sides are merely Equations (1.3) and (1.4) multiplied by −1. Following is a sample trade that applies the long call profit formula.

Example trade: A call with 45 DTE duration is traded on an underlying that is currently priced at $100 ($S$). The strike price is $105 ($K$), and the long call is currently valued at $100 per one lot ($1 per share).

- Scenario 1: The underlying increases to $105 by the expiration date.
  - Long call P/L: 100 shares · (($105 − $105) − $1) = −$100;
  - Short call P/L: +$100.

---

[2] The future value of the option should be used, but for simplicity, this approximates the future value as the current price of the option. The future value of the option premium is the current value of the option multiplied by the time-adjusted interest rate factor.

- Scenario 2: The underlying increases to $110 by the expiration date.
  - Long call P/L: 100 shares · (($110 − $105) − $1) = +$400;
  - Short call P/L: −$400.
- Scenario 3: The underlying decreases to $95 by the expiration date.
  - Long call P/L: 100 Shares · ($0 − $1) = −$100;
  - Short call P/L: +$100.

The trader adopting the long position pays the seller the option premium upfront and profits when the intrinsic value exceeds the price of the contract. The short trader profits when the intrinsic value remains below the price of the contract, especially when the position expires worthless (no intrinsic value). The extrinsic value of an option generally decreases over the duration of the contract, as uncertainty around the underlying price and uncertainty around the profit potential of the option decrease. As a position nears expiration, the price of an option converges toward its intrinsic value.

Options pricing clearly plays a large role in options trading. To develop an intuitive understanding around how options are priced, understanding the mathematical assumptions around market efficiency and price dynamics is critical.

The Efficient Market Hypothesis

Traders must make a number of assumptions prior to placing a trade. Options traders must make directional assumptions about the price of the underlying over a given time frame: bearish (expecting price to decrease), bullish (expecting price to increase), or neutral (expecting price to remain relatively unchanged). Options traders also must make assumptions about the current value of an option. If options contracts are perceived as overvalued, long positions are less likely to profit. If options contracts are perceived as undervalued, short positions are less likely to profit. These assumptions about underlying and option price dynamics are a personal choice, but traders can formulate consistent assumptions by referring to the efficient market hypothesis (EMH). The EMH states that instruments are traded at a fair price, and the current price of an asset reflects some amount of available information. The hypothesis comes in three forms:

1. **Weak EMH:** Current prices reflect all past price information.

2. Semi-strong EMH: Current prices reflect all publicly available information.

3. Strong EMH: Current prices reflect all possible information.

No variant of the EMH is universally accepted or rejected. The form that a trader assumes is subjective, and methods of market analysis available are limited depending on that choice. Proponents of the strong EMH posit that investors benefit from investing in low-cost passive index funds because the market is unbeatable. Opponents believe the market is beatable by exploiting inefficiencies in the market. Traders who accept the weak EMH believe technical analysis (using past price trends to predict future price trends) is invalidated, but fundamental analysis (using related economic data to predict future price trends) is still viable. Traders who accept the semi-strong EMH assume fundamental analysis would not yield systematic success but trading according to private information would. Traders who accept the strong EMH maintain that even insider trading will not result in consistent success and no exploitable market inefficiencies are available to anyone.

This book focuses on highly liquid markets, and inefficiencies are assumed to be minimal. More specifically, this book assumes a semi-strong form of the EMH. Rather than constructing portfolios according to forecasts of future price trends, the purpose of this text is to demonstrate how trading options according to current market conditions and directional *volatility* assumptions (rather than price assumptions) has allowed options sellers to consistently outperform the market.

This "edge" is not the result of some inherent market inefficiency but rather a trade-off of risk. Recall the example long call trade from the previous section. Notice that there are more scenarios in which the short trader profits compared to the long trader. Generally, short premium positions are more likely to yield a profit compared to long premium positions. This is because options are assumed to be priced efficiently and scaled according to the perceived risk in the market, meaning that long positions only profit when the underlying has large directional moves outside of expectations. As these types of events are uncommon, options contracts go unused the majority of the time and short premium positions profit more often than long positions. However, when those large, unexpected moves *do* occur, the short premium positions are subject to potentially massive losses. The risk profiles for options are complex, but they can be intuitively represented with probability distributions.

Probability Distributions

To better understand the risk profiles of short options, this book utilizes basic concepts from probability theory, specifically random variables and probability distributions. Random variables are formal stand-ins for uncertain quantities. The probability distribution of a random variable describes possible values of that quantity and the likelihood of each value occurring. Generally, probability distributions are represented by the symbol P, which can be read as "the probability that." For example, P (a fair coin flips heads) $= 1/2$. Random variables and probability distributions are tools for working with probabilistic systems (i.e., systems with many unpredictable outcomes), such as stock prices. Although future outcomes cannot be precisely predicted, understanding the distribution of a probabilistic system makes it possible to form expectations about the future, including the uncertainty associated with those expectations.

Let's begin with an example of a simple probabilistic system: rolling a pair of fair, six-sided dice. In this case, if D represents the sum of the dice, then D is a random variable with 11 possible values ranging from 2 to 12. Some of these outcomes are more likely than others. Since, for instance, there are more ways to roll a sum of 7 ([1,6], [2,5], [3,4], [4,3], [5,2], [6,1]) than a sum of 10 ([4,6], [5,5], [6,4]), there is a higher probability of rolling a 7 than a 10. Observing that there are 36 possible rolls ([1,1], [1,2], [2,1], etc.) and that each is equally likely, one can use symbols to be more precise about this:

$$P(D = 7) = 6/36 \approx 16.67\% \text{ while } P(D = 10) = 3/36 \approx 8.33\%$$

The distribution of D can be represented elegantly using a histogram. These types of graphs display the frequency of different outcomes, grouped according to defined ranges. When working with measured data, histograms are used to estimate the true underlying probability distribution of a probabilistic system. For this fair dice example, there will be 11 bins, corresponding to the 11 possible outcomes. This histogram is shown below in Figure 1.1, populated with data from 100,000 simulated dice rolls.

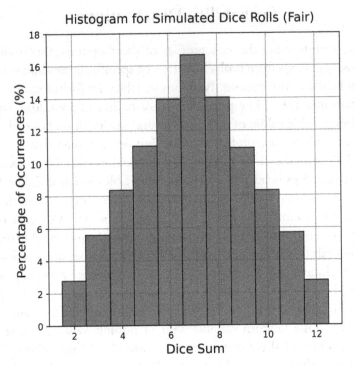

Figure 1.1 A histogram for 100,000 simulated rolls for a pair of fair dice. This diagram shows the likelihood of each outcome occurring according to this simulation (e.g., the height of the bin ranging from 6.5 to 7.5 is near 17%, indicating that 7 occurred nearly 17% of the time in the 100,000 trials).

Distributions like the ones shown here can be summarized using quantitative measures called *moments*.[3] The first two moments are mean and variance.

Mean (first moment): Also known as the average and represented by the Greek letter μ (mu), this value describes the central tendency of

---

[3] Population calculations are used for all the moments introduced throughout this chapter.

a distribution. This is calculated by summing all the observed outcomes $(x_1, x_2, \cdots, x_n)$ together and dividing by the number of observations (n):

$$\text{Mean} = \mu = \frac{1}{n} \cdot \sum_{i=1}^{n} x_i = \frac{1}{n} \cdot (x_1 + x_2 + x_3 + \cdots + x_n) \qquad (1.5)$$

For distributions based on statistical observations with *a sufficiently large number of occurrences*, the mean corresponds to the expected value of that distribution. The expected value of a random variable is the weighted average of outcomes and the anticipated average outcome over future trials. The expected value of a random variable X, denoted $E[X]$, can be estimated using statistical data and Equation (1.5), *or if* the unique outcomes $(x_1, x_2, \cdots x_k)$ and their respective probabilities $p_i = P(X = x_i)$ are known, then the expected value can also be calculated using the following formula:

$$E[X] = \sum_{i=1}^{k} x_i \cdot p_i = x_1 \cdot p_1 + x_2 \cdot p_2 + x_3 \cdot p_3 + \cdots + x_k \cdot p_k \qquad (1.6)$$

In the dice sum example, represented with random variable D, the possible outcomes (2, 3, 4, ..., 12) and the probability of each occurring (2.78%, 5.56%, 8.33%, ..., 2.78%) are known, so the expected value can be determined as follows:

$$E[D] = 2 \cdot 2.78\% + 3 \cdot 5.56\% + 4 \cdot 8.33\% + \cdots + 12 \cdot 2.78\% = 7$$

The theoretical long-term average sum is seven. Therefore, if this experiment is repeated many times, the mean of the observations calculated using Equation (1.5) should yield an output close to seven.

Variance (second moment): This is the measure of the spread, or variation, of the data points from the mean of the distribution. Standard deviation, represented with by the Greek letter σ (sigma), is the square root of variance and is commonly used as a measure of uncertainty (equivalently, risk or volatility). Distributions with more variance are wider and have more uncertainty around future outcomes. Variance is calculated according to the following:[4]

$$\text{Variance} = \sigma^2 = \frac{1}{n} \cdot \sum_{i=1}^{n} (x_i - \mu)^2 \qquad (1.7)$$

---

[4] This is the sum of the squared differences between each data point and the distribution mean, normalized by the number of data points in the set.

When a large portion of data points are dispersed far from the mean, the variance of the entire set is large, and uncertainty on measurements from that system is significant. The variance of a random variable X, denoted Var(X), can also be calculated in terms of the expected value, $E[X]$:

$$Var(X) = E[(X - E[X])^2] = E[X^2] - E[X]^2$$

$$= (x_1^2 \cdot p_1 + x_2^2 \cdot p_2 + x_3^2 \cdot p_3 + \cdots + x_k^2 \cdot p_k)$$

$$- (x_1 \cdot p_1 + x_2 \cdot p_2 + x_3 \cdot p_3 + \cdots + x_k \cdot p_k)^2 \qquad (1.8)$$

For the dice sum random variable, D, the possible outcomes (2, 3, 4, ..., 12) and the probability of each occurring (2.78%, 5.56%, 8.33%, ..., 2.78%) are known, so the variance of this experiment is as follows:

$$Var(D) = (2^2 \cdot 2.78\% + 3^2 \cdot 5.56\% + 4^2 \cdot 8.33\% + \ldots + 12^2$$

$$\cdot\, 2.78\%) - (7)^2 \approx 5.84$$

This equation indicates that the spread of the distribution for this random variable is around 5.84 and the uncertainty (standard deviation) is approximately 2.4 (shown in Figure 1.2).

One can compare these theoretical estimates for the mean and standard deviation of the dice sum experiment to the values measured from statistical data. The calculated first and second moments from the simulated dice roll experiment are plotted in Figure 1.2 for comparison.

Obtaining a distribution average near 7.0 makes intuitive sense because 7 is the most likely sum to roll out of the possible outcomes. The standard deviation indicates that the uncertainty associated with that expected value is near 2.4. Inferring from the shape of the distribution, which has most of the probability mass concentrated near the center, one can conclude that on any given roll the outcome will most likely fall between five and nine.

The distribution just shown is symmetric about the mean, but probability distributions are often asymmetric. To quantify the degree of asymmetry for a distribution, the third moment is used.

Skew (third moment): This is a measure of the asymmetry of a distribution. A distribution's skew can be positive, negative, or zero and depends on whether the tail to the right of the mean is larger (positive

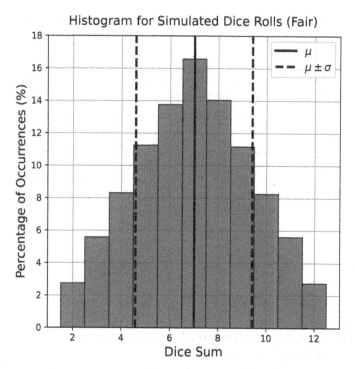

Figure 1.2 A histogram for 100,000 simulated dice rolls with fair dice. Included is the mean of the distribution (solid line) and the standard deviation of the distribution on either side of the mean (dotted line), both calculated using the observations from the simulated experiment. The average of this distribution was 7.0 and the standard deviation was 2.4, consistent with the theoretical estimates.

skew), to the left is larger (negative skew), or equal on both sides (zero skew). Unlike mean and standard deviation, which have units defined by the random variable, skew is a pure number that quantifies the degree of asymmetry according to the following formula:

$$\text{Skew} = \frac{1}{n} \cdot \frac{\sum_{i=1}^{n} (x_i - \mu)^3}{\sigma^3} \qquad (1.9)$$

The concept of skew and its applications can be best understood with a modification to the dice rolling example. Suppose that the dice are biased rather than fair. Let's consider two scenarios: a pair of unfair dice with a small number bias (two and three more likely) and a pair of unfair dice with a large number bias (four and five more likely).

The probabilities of each number appearing on each die for the different cases are shown in Table 1.2.

Table 1.2   The probability of each number appearing on each die in the three different scenarios, one fair and two unfair.

| | Probability of Number Appearing on Each Die | | |
Die Number	Fair	Unfair (Small Number Bias)	Unfair (Large Number Bias)
1	16.67%	10%	10%
2	16.67%	30%	10%
3	16.67%	30%	10%
4	16.67%	10%	30%
5	16.67%	10%	30%
6	16.67%	10%	10%

When rolling the *fair* pair and plotting the histogram of the possible sums, the distribution is symmetric about the mean and has a skew of zero. However, the distributions when rolling the unfair dice are skewed, as shown in Figures 1.3(a) and (b).

The skew of a distribution is classified according to where the majority of the distribution mass is concentrated. Remember that the positive side is to the right of the mean and the negative side is to the left. The histogram in Figure 1.3(a) has a longer tail on the positive side and has the most mass concentrated on the negative side of the mean: This is an example of *positive* skew (skew = 0.45). The histogram in Figure 1.3(b) has a longer tail on the negative side and has the majority of the mass concentrated on the positive side of the mean: This is an example of *negative* skew (skew = −0.45).

When a distribution has skew, the interpretation of standard deviation changes. In the example with fair dice, the expected value of the experiment is 7.0 ± 2.4, suggesting that any given trial will most likely have an outcome between five and nine. This is a valid interpretation because the distribution is symmetric about the mean and most of the distribution mass is concentrated around it. However, consider the distribution in the unfair example with the large number bias. This distribution has a mean of 7.8 and a standard deviation of 2.0, naively suggesting that the outcome will most likely be between six and nine

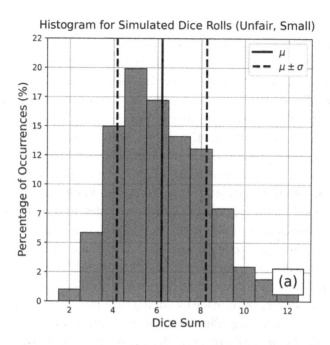

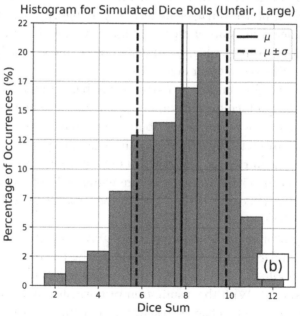

Figure 1.3 (a) A histogram for 100,000 simulated dice rolls with unfair dice, biased such that smaller numbers (2 and 3) are more likely to appear on each die. (b) A histogram for 100,000 simulated dice rolls with unfair dice, biased such that larger numbers (4 and 5) are more likely to appear on each die.

with the outcomes on either side being equally probable. However, because the majority of the occurrences are concentrated on the positive side of the mean (roughly 60% of occurrences), the uncertainty is not symmetric. This concept will be discussed in more detail in a later chapter, as distributions of financial instruments are commonly skewed, and there is ambiguity in defining risk under those circumstances.

Mathematicians and scientists have encountered some probability distributions repeatedly in theory and applications. These distributions have, in turn, received a great deal of study. Assuming the underlying distribution of an experiment resembles a well known form can often greatly simplify statistical analysis. The normal distribution (also known as the Gaussian distribution or the bell curve) is arguably one of the most well-known probability distributions and foundational in quantitative finance. It describes countless different real-world systems because of a result known as the central limit theorem. This theorem says, roughly, that if a random variable is made by adding together many independently random pieces, then, regardless of what those pieces are, the result will be normally distributed. For example, the distribution in the two-dice example is fairly non-normal, being relatively triangular and lacking tails. If one considered the sum of more and more dice, each of which is an independent random variable, the distribution would gradually take on a bell shape. This is shown in Figure 1.4.

The normal distribution is a symmetric, bell-shaped distribution, meaning that equidistant events on either side of the center are equally likely and the skew is zero. The distribution is centered around the mean, and outcomes further away from the mean are less likely. The normal distribution has the intriguing property that 68% of occurrences fall within $\pm 1\sigma$ of the mean, 95% of occurrences are within $\pm 2\sigma$ of the mean, and 99.7% of occurrences are within $\pm 3\sigma$ of the mean. Figure 1.5 plots a normal distribution.

These probabilities can be used to roughly contextualize distributions with similar geometry. For example, in the fair dice pair model, the expected value of the fair dice experiment was 7.0, and the standard deviation was 2.4. With the assumption of normality, one would infer there is roughly a 68% chance that future outcomes will fall between five and nine. The true probability is 66.67% for this random variable,

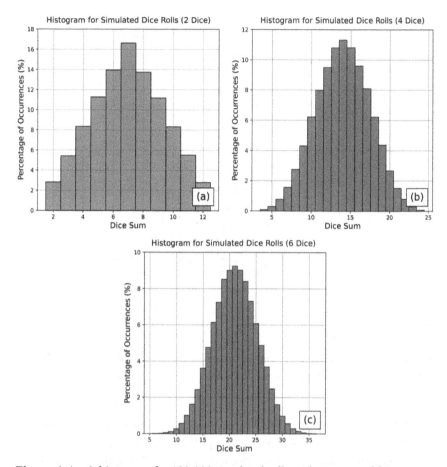

Figure 1.4 A histogram for 100,000 simulated rolls with a group of fair, six-sided dice numbering (a) 2, (b) 4, or (c) 6.

indicating that the normality assumption is not exactly correct but can be used for the purposes of approximation. As more dice are added to the example, this approximation becomes increasingly accurate.

Understanding distribution statistics and the properties of the normal distribution is incredibly useful in quantitative finance. The expected return of a stock is usually estimated by the mean return, and the historic risk is estimated with the standard deviation of returns (historical volatility). Stock log returns are also widely assumed to be normally distributed. Although, this is only approximately true because the overwhelming

The Normal Distribution

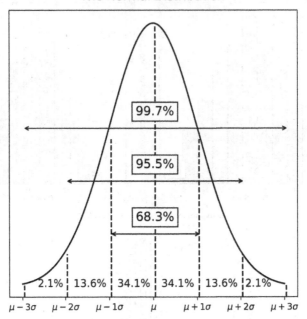

Figure 1.5 A detailed plot of the normal distribution and the corresponding probabilities at each standard deviation mark.

majority of stocks and ETFs have skewed returns distributions.[5] Regardless, this normality estimation provides a quantitative framework for expectations around future price moments. This approximation also simplifies mathematical models of price dynamics and options pricing, the most notable of which is the Black–Scholes model.

The Black–Scholes Model

The Black–Scholes options pricing formalism revolutionized options markets when it was published in 1973. It provided the first popular quantitative framework for estimating the fair price of an option

---

[5] The skew of the returns distribution is also used to estimate the directional risk of an asset. The fourth moment (kurtosis) quantifies how heavy the tails of a returns distribution are and is commonly used to estimate the outlier risk of an asset.

according to the contract parameters and the characteristics of the underlying. The Black-Scholes equation models the price evolution of a European-style option (an option that can only be exercised at expiration) within the context of the broader financial market. The corresponding Black-Scholes formula uses this equation to estimate the theoretical price of that option according to its parameters.

It's important to note that the purpose of this Black-Scholes section is *not* to elucidate the underlying mathematics of the model, which can be quite complicated. The output of the model is merely a theoretical value for the fair price of an option. In practice, an option's price typically deviates from this value because of market speculation and supply and demand, which this model does not take into account. Rather, it is essential to have at least a superficial grasp of the Black-Scholes model to understand (1) the foundational assumptions of financial markets and (2) where implied volatility (a gauge for the market's *perception* of risk) comes from.

The Black-Scholes model is based on a set of assumptions related to the dynamics of financial assets and the market as a whole. The assumptions are as follows:

- The market is frictionless (i.e., there are no transaction fees).
- Cash can be borrowed and lent in any amount, even fractional, at the risk-free rate (the theoretical rate of return of an investment with no risk, a macroeconomic variable assumed to be constant).
- There is no arbitrage opportunity (i.e., profits in excess of the risk-free rate cannot be made without risk).
- Stocks can be bought and sold in any amount, even fractional amounts.
- Stocks do not pay dividends.[6]
- Stock log returns follow Brownian motion with constant drift and volatility (the theoretical mean and standard deviation of annual log returns).

A Brownian motion, or a Wiener process, is a type of stochastic process or a system that experiences random fluctuations as it evolves with time. Traditionally used to describe the positional fluctuations of a

---

[6] Dividends can be accounted for in variants of the original model.

particle suspended in fluid at thermal equilibrium,[7] a standard Wiener process (denoted $W(t)$) is mathematically defined by the conditions in the grey box. The mathematical definition can be overlooked if preferred, as the intuition behind the mathematics is more crucial for understanding the theoretical foundation of options pricing and follows after.

- $W(0) = 0$ (i.e., the process initially begins at location 0).
- $W(t)$ is almost surely continuous.
- The increments of $W(t)$, defined as $W(t) - W(s)$ where $0 < s < t$, are normally distributed with mean 0 and variance $t - s$ (i.e., the steps of the Wiener process are normally distributed with constant mean of 0 and variance of Δt).
- Disjoint increments of $W(t)$ are independent of one another (i.e., the current step of the process is not influenced by the previous steps, nor does it influence the subsequent steps).

Simplified, a Wiener process is a process that follows a random path. Each step in this path is probabilistic and independent of one another. When disjoint steps of equal duration are plotted in a histogram, that distribution is normal with a constant mean and variance. Brownian motion dynamics are driven by this underlying process. These conditions can be best understood visually, which will also demonstrate why this assumption appears in the development of the Black-Scholes model as an approximation for price dynamics. Figures 1.6 and 1.7 illustrate the characteristics of Brownian motion, and Figure 1.8 illustrates the dynamics of SPY from 2010–2015[8] for the purposes of comparison.

The price trends of SPY in Figure 1.8(b) appear fairly similar to the Brownian motion cumulative horizontal displacements shown in Figure 1.6(c). The daily returns for SPY are more prone to outlier moves

---

[7] This application of Wiener processes as well as their use in financial mathematics are due to them arising as the scaling limit of simple random walk. A simple random walk is a discrete process that takes independent ±1 steps with probability 1/2. The scaling limit is reached by shrinking the size of the steps while speeding up their rate in such a way that the process neither sits at its initial location nor runs off to infinity immediately.

[8] Note that, unless stated or shown otherwise, the date ranges throughout this book generally end on the first of the final year. For the range shown here, the data begins on January 1, 2010 and ends on January 1, 2015.

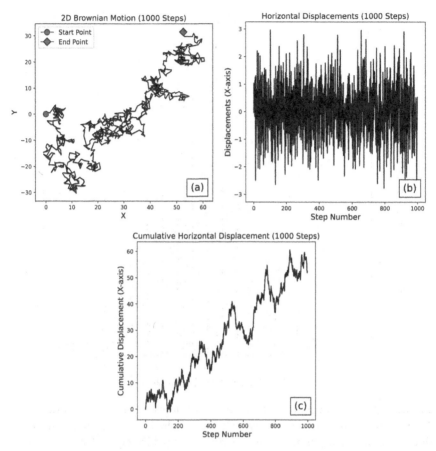

Figure 1.6 (a) The 2D position of a particle in a fluid, moving with Brownian motion. The particle begins at a coordinate of $(X = 0, \ Y = 0)$ and drifts to a new location over 1,000 steps. (b) The horizontal displacements[9] of the particle (i.e., the movements of the particle along the X-axis over 1,000 steps). (c) The cumulative horizontal displacement of the particle over 1,000 steps.

compared to the horizontal displacements of Brownian motion but share some characteristics. The symmetric geometry of the SPY returns histogram bears resemblance to the fairly normal distribution of horizontal displacements, with the tails of the distribution being more prominent as a result of the history of large price moves.

Similarities are clear between price dynamics and Brownian motion, but this remains a highly simplified model of price dynamics.

---

[9] Displacement along the X-axis is the difference between the current horizontal location of the particle and the previous horizontal location of the particle for each step.

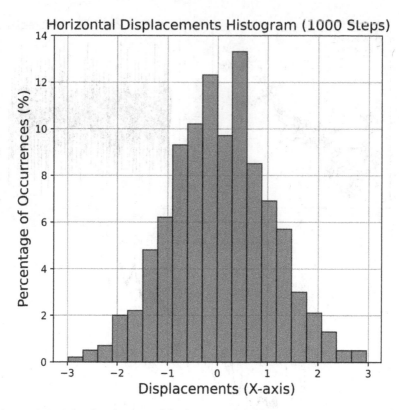

Figure 1.7   The distribution of the horizontal displacements of the particle over 1,000 steps. As characteristic of a Wiener process, the increments are normally distributed, have a mean of zero and variance $t - s$ (which equals 1 in this case). This figure indicates that horizontal step sizes between –1 and 1 are most common, and step sizes with a larger magnitude than 1 are less common.

In reality, stock log returns are not normal and are typically skewed to the upside or downside, depending on the specific underlying. Additionally, the drift and volatility of a stock are not directly observable, and it cannot be experimentally confirmed whether or not these variables are constant. Stock volatility approximated with historical return data is rarely constant with time (a phenomenon known as heteroscedasticity). Stock returns are also not typically independent of one another across time (a phenomenon known as autocorrelation), which is a requirement for this model.

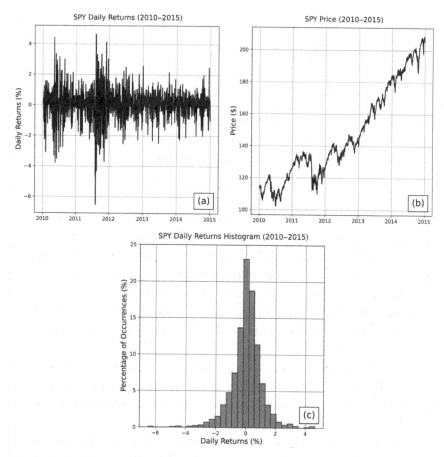

Figure 1.8 The (a) daily returns, (b) price, and (c) daily returns histogram for SPY from 2010–2015.

Although the normality assumption is not entirely accurate, making this simplification allows the development of the rest of this theoretical framework shown in the gray box. The formalism in the gray box is supplemental material for the mathematically inclined. The interpretation of the math, which is more significant, follows after. It should be noted that the Black-Scholes model technically assumes that stock prices follow *geometric Brownian motion*, which is more accurate because price movements cannot be negative. Geometric Brownian motion is a slight modification of Brownian motion and requires that the logarithm of the signal follow

Brownian motion rather than the signal itself. As it relates to price dynamics, this suggests that the log returns are normally distributed with constant drift (return rate) and volatility.[10]

For the price of a stock that follows a geometric Brownian motion, the dynamics of the asset price can be represented with the following stochastic differential equation:[11]

$$dS(t) = S(t)(\mu dt + \sigma dW(t)) \qquad (1.10)$$

where $S(t)$ is the price of the stock at time t, $W(t)$ is the Wiener process at time t, μ is a drift rate, and σ is the volatility of the stock. The drift rate and volatility of the stock are assumed to be constant, and it's important to reiterate that neither of these variables are directly observable. These constants can be approximated using the average return of a stock and the standard deviation of historical returns, but they can never be precisely known.

The equation states that each stock price increment ($dS(t)$) is driven by a predictable amount of drift (with expected return μdt) and some amount of random noise ($\sigma dW(t)$). In other words, this equation has two components: one that models *deterministic* price trends ($S(t)\mu dt$) and one that models probabilistic price fluctuations ($S(t)\sigma dW(t)$). The important takeaway from this observation is that inherent uncertainty is in the price of stock, represented with the contributions from the

---

[10] Simple returns will also be approximated as normally distributed throughout this book. Although this is not explicitly implied by the Black-Scholes model, it is a fair and intuitive approximation in most cases because the difference between log returns and simple returns is typically negligible on daily timescales.

[11] d is a symbol used in calculus to represent a mathematical derivative. It equivalently represents an infinitesimal change in the variable it's applied to. $dS(t)$ is merely a very small, incremental movement of the stock price at time t. ∂ is the partial derivative, which also represents a very small change in one variable with respect to variations in another.

Wiener process. Because the increments of a Wiener process are independent of one another, it also is common to assume that the weak EMH holds at minimum, in addition to the normality of log returns.

Using this equation as a basis for the derivation, assuming a riskless options portfolio must earn the risk-free rate, and rearranging terms, the Black-Scholes equation follows:

$$\frac{\partial C}{\partial t} + rS\left(\frac{\partial C}{\partial S}\right) + \frac{1}{2}\sigma^2 S^2 \left(\frac{\partial^2 C}{\partial S^2}\right) = rC \qquad (1.11)$$

where C is the price of a European call (with a dependence on S and t), S is the price of the stock (with a dependence on t), r is the risk-free rate, and σ is the volatility of the stock. The Black-Scholes formula can be calculated by solving the Black-Scholes equation according to boundary conditions given by the payoff at expiration of European options. The formula, which provides the value of a European call option for a non-dividend-paying stock, is given by the following equation:

$$C(S, t) = N(d_1)S(t) - N(d_2)Ke^{-r(T-t)} \qquad (1.12)$$

where $N(d_1)$ is the value of the standard normal cumulative distribution function at d_1 and similarly for $N(d_2)$, T is the time that the option will expire ($T - t$ is the duration of the contract), $S(t)$ is the price of the stock at time t, K is the strike price of the option, and d_1 and d_2 are given by the following:

$$d_1 = \frac{1}{\sigma\sqrt{T-t}}\left[\ln\left(\frac{S(t)}{K}\right) + \left(r + \frac{1}{2}\sigma^2\right)(T - t)\right] \qquad (1.13)$$

$$d_2 = d_1 - \sigma\sqrt{T-t} \qquad (1.14)$$

where σ is the volatility of the stock. If the equations seem gross, it's because they are.

Again, the purpose of this section is not to describe the underlying mechanics of the Black–Scholes model in detail. Rather, Equations (1.10) through (1.14) are included to emphasize three important points.

1. There is inherent uncertainty in the price of stock. Stock price movements are also assumed to be independent of one another and log-normally distributed.[12]
2. An estimate for the fair price of an option can be calculated according to the price of the stock, the volatility of the stock, the risk-free rate, the duration of the contract, and the strike price.
3. The volatility of a stock, which plays an important role in estimating the risk of an asset and the valuation of an option, cannot be directly observed. This suggests that the "true risk" of an instrument can never be exactly known. Risk can only be approximated using a metric, such as historical volatility or the standard deviation of the historical returns over some timescale, typically matching the duration of the contract. Other than using a past-looking metric, such as historical volatility to estimate the risk of an asset, one can also infer the risk of an asset from the price of its options.

As stated previously, the Black–Scholes model only gives a *theoretical* estimate for the fair price of an option. Once the contract is traded on the options market, the price of the contract is often driven up or down depending on speculation and perceived risk. The deviation of an option's price from its theoretical value as a result of these external factors is indicative of *implied volatility*. When initially valuing an option, the historical volatility of the stock has been priced into the model. However, when the price of the option trades higher or lower than its theoretical value, this indicates that the *perceived* volatility of the underlying deviates from what is estimated by historical returns.

Implied volatility may be the most important metric in options trading. It is effectively a measure of the *sentiment* of risk for a given underlying according to the supply and demand for options contracts. For an example, suppose a non–dividend-paying stock currently trading at $100 per share has a historical 45-day returns volatility of 20%. Suppose its call option with a 45-day duration and a strike price of $105 is trading at

---

[12] The log function and log-normal distribution are both covered in the appendix.

$2 per share. Plugging these parameters into the Black-Scholes model, this call option should theoretically be trading at $1 per share. However, demand for this position has increased the contract price significantly. For the model to return a call price of $2 per share, the volatility of this underlying would have to be 28% (assuming all else is constant). Therefore, although the historical volatility of the underlying is only 20%, the perceived risk of that underlying (i.e., the implied volatility) is actually 28%.

To conclude, the primary purpose of this section was not to dive into the math of the Black-Scholes. These concepts were, instead, introduced to justify the following axioms that are foundational to this book:

- Profits cannot be made without risk.
- Stock log returns have inherent uncertainty and are assumed to follow a normal distribution.
- Stock price movements are independent across time (i.e., future price changes are independent of past price changes, requiring a minimum of the weak EMH).
- Options can theoretically be priced fairly based on the price of the stock, the volatility of the stock, the risk-free rate, the duration of the contract, and the strike price.
- The volatility of an asset cannot be directly observed, only estimated using metrics like historical volatility or implied volatility.

The Greeks

Other than implied volatility, the Greeks are the most relevant metrics derived from the Black-Scholes model. The Greeks are a set of risk measures, and each describes the sensitivity of an option's price with respect to changes in some variable. The most essential Greeks for options traders are delta (Δ), gamma (Γ), and theta (θ).

Delta (Δ) is one of the most important and widely used Greeks. It is a first-order[13] Greek that measures the expected change in the option

---

[13] Order refers to the number of mathematical derivatives taken on the price of the option. Delta has a single derivative of V and is first-order. Greeks of second-order are reached by taking a derivative of first-order Greeks.

price given a $1 increase in the price of the underlying (assuming all other variables stay constant). The equation is as follows:

$$\Delta = \frac{\partial V}{\partial S} \tag{1.15}$$

where V is the price of the option (a call or a put) and S is the price of the underlying stock, noting that ∂ is the partial derivative. The value of delta ranges from -1 to 1, and the sign of delta depends on the type of position:

- Long stock: Δ is 1.
- Long call and short put: Δ is between 0 and 1.
- Long put and short call: Δ is between -1 and 0.

For example, the price of a long call option with a delta of 0.50 (denoted 50Δ because that is the total Δ for a one lot, or 100 shares of underlying) will increase by approximately $0.50 per share when the price of the underlying increases by $1. This makes intuitive sense because a long stock, a long call, and a short put are all bullish strategies, meaning they will profit when the underlying price increases. Similarly, because long puts and short calls are bearish, they will take a loss when the underlying price increases.

Delta has a sign and magnitude, so it is a measure of the *degree* of *directional risk* of a position. The sign of delta indicates the direction of the risk, and the magnitude of delta indicates the severity of exposure. The larger the magnitude of delta, the larger the profit and loss potential of the contract. This is because positions with larger deltas are closer to/deeper ITM and more sensitive to changes in the underlying price. A contract with a delta of 1.0 (100Δ) has maximal directional exposure and is maximally ITM. 100Δ options behave like the stock price, as a $1 increase in the underlying creates a $1 increase in the option's price per share. A contract with a delta of 0.0 has no directional exposure and is maximally OTM. A 50Δ contract is defined as having the ATM strike.[14]

Because delta is a measure of directional exposure, it plays a large role when hedging directional risks. For instance, if a trader currently has a 50Δ position on and wants the position to be relatively insensitive to

---

[14] In practice, the strike and underlying prices for 50Δ contracts tend to differ *slightly* due to strike skew.

directional moves in the underlying, the trader could offset that exposure with the addition of 50 negative deltas (e.g., two 25Δ long puts). The composite position is called delta neutral.

Gamma (Γ) is a second-order Greek and a measure of the expected change in the option *delta* given a $1 change in the underlying price. Gamma is mathematically represented as follows:

$$\Gamma = \frac{\partial \Delta}{\partial S} = \frac{\partial^2 V}{\partial S^2} \qquad (1.16)$$

As with delta, the sign of gamma depends on the type of position:

- Long call and long put: $\Gamma > 0$.
- Short call and short put: $\Gamma < 0$.

In other words, if there is a $1 increase in the underlying price, then the delta for all long positions will become more positive, and the delta for all short positions will become more negative. This makes intuitive sense because a $1 increase in the underlying pushes long calls further ITM, increasing the directional exposure of the contract, and it pushes long puts further OTM, decreasing the inverse directional exposure of the contract and bringing the negative delta closer to zero. The magnitude of gamma is highest for ATM positions and lower for ITM and OTM positions, meaning that delta is most sensitive to underlying price movements at -50Δ and 50Δ.

Awareness of gamma is critical when trading options, particularly when aiming for specific directional exposure. The delta of a contract is typically transient, so the gamma of a position gives a better indication of the long-term directional exposure. Suppose traders wanted to construct a delta neutral position by pairing a short call (negative delta) with a short put (positive delta), and they are considering using 20Δ or 40Δ contracts (all other parameters identical). The 40Δ contracts are much closer to ATM (50Δ) and have more profit potential than the 20Δ positions, but they also have significantly more gamma risk and are less likely to remain delta neutral in the long term. The optimal choice would then depend on how much risk traders are willing to accept and their profit goals. For traders with high profit goals and a large enough account to handle the large P/L swings and loss potential of the trade, the 40Δ contracts are more suitable.

Theta (θ) is a first-order Greek that measures the expected P/L changes resulting from the decay of the option's extrinsic value (the difference between the current market price for the option and the intrinsic value of the option) per day. It is also commonly referred to as the time decay of the option. Theta is mathematically represented as follows:

$$\theta = \frac{\partial V}{\partial t} \tag{1.17}$$

where V is the price of the option (a call or a put) and t is time. The sign of theta depends on the type of position and is opposite gamma:

- Long call and long put: $\theta < 0$.
- Short call and short put: $\theta > 0$.

In other words, the time decay of the extrinsic value decreases the value of the long position and increases the value of the short position. For instance, a long call with a theta of −5 per one lot is expected to decline in value by $5 per day. This makes intuitive sense because the holders of the contract take gradual losses as their asset depreciates with time, a result of the value of the option converging to its intrinsic value as uncertainty dissipates. Because the extrinsic value of a contract decreases with time, the short side of the position profits with time and experiences positive time decay. The magnitude of theta is highest for ATM options and lower for ITM and OTM positions, all else constant.

There is a trade-off between the gamma and theta of a position. For instance, a long call with the benefit of a large, positive gamma will also be subjected to a large amount of negative time decay. Consider these examples:

- **Position 1:** A 45 DTE, 16Δ call with a strike price of $50 is trading on a $45 underlying. The long position has a gamma of 5.4 and a theta of −1.3.
- **Position 2:** A 45 DTE, 44Δ call with a strike price of $50 is trading on a $49 underlying. The long position has a gamma of 7.9 and a theta of −2.2.

Compared to the first position, the second position has more gamma exposure, meaning that the contract delta (and the contract price) is more sensitive to changes in the underlying price and is more likely to move ITM. However, this position also comes with more theta decay, meaning that the extrinsic value also decreases more rapidly with time.

To conclude this discussion of the Black-Scholes model and its risk measures, note that the outputs of all options pricing models should be taken with a grain of salt. Pricing models are founded on simplified assumptions of real financial markets. Those assumptions tend to become less representative in highly volatile market conditions when potential profits and losses become much larger. The assumptions and Greeks of the Black-Scholes model can be used to form reasonable expectations around risk and return *in most market conditions*, but it's also important to supplement that framework with model-free statistics.

Covariance and Correlation

Up until now we have discussed trading with respect to a single position, but quantifying the relationships between multiple positions is equally important. Covariance quantifies how two signals move relative to their means with respect to one another. It is an effective way to measure the variability between two variables. For one signal, X, with observations $(x_1, x_2, \cdots, x_n)$ and mean μ_X, and another, Y, with observations $(y_1, y_2, \cdots, y_n)$ and mean μ_Y, the covariance between the two signals is given by the following:

$$\text{Covariance} = \text{Cov}(X, Y) = \frac{1}{n} \cdot \sum_{i=1}^{n} (x_i - \mu_X)(y_i - \mu_Y) \qquad (1.18)$$

Represented in terms of random variables X and Y, this is equivalent to the following:[15]

$$\text{Cov}(X, Y) = E[(X - E[X])(Y - E[Y])] \qquad (1.19)$$

Simplified, covariance quantifies the tendency of the linear relationship between two variables:

- A *positive* covariance indicates that the high values of one signal coincide with the high values of the other and likewise for the low values of each signal.

---

[15] The covariance of a variable with itself (e.g., Cov(X, X)) is merely the variance of the signal itself.

- A *negative* covariance indicates that the high values of one signal coincide with the low values of the other and vice versa.
- A covariance of zero indicates that no linear trend was observed between the two variables.

Covariance can be best understood with a graphical example. Consider the following ETFs with daily returns shown in the following figures: SPY (S&P 500), QQQ (Nasdaq 100), and GLD (Gold), TLT (20+ Year Treasury Bonds).

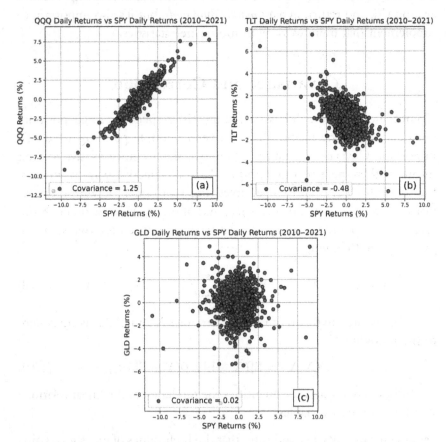

Figure 1.9 (a) QQQ returns versus SPY returns. The covariance between these assets is 1.25, indicating that these instruments tend to move similarly. (b) TLT returns versus SPY returns. The covariance between these assets is −0.48, indicating that they tend to move inversely of one another. (c) GLD returns versus SPY returns. The covariance between these assets is 0.02, indicating that there is not a strong linear relationship between these variables.

Covariance measures the direction of the linear relationship between two variables, but it does not give a clear notion of the *strength* of that relationship. Because the covariance between two variables is specific to the scale of those variables, the covariances between two sets of pairs are not comparable. Correlation, however, is a normalized covariance that indicates the direction *and* strength of the linear relationship, and it is also invariant to scale. For signals X, Y with standard deviations σ_X, σ_Y and covariance $Cov(X, Y)$, the correlation coefficient ρ (rho) is given by the following:

$$\text{Correlation} = \rho_{XY} = \frac{Cov(X, Y)}{\sigma_X \sigma_Y} \tag{1.20}$$

The correlation coefficient ranges from -1 to 1, with 1 corresponding to a perfect positive linear relationship, -1 corresponding to a perfect negative linear relationship, and 0 corresponding to no measured linear relationship. Revisiting the example pairs shown in Figure 1.9, the strength of the linear relationship in each case can now be evaluated and compared.

For Figure 1.9(a), QQQ returns versus SPY returns, the correlation between these assets is 0.88, indicating a strong, positive linear relationship. For Figure 1.9(b), TLT returns versus SPY returns, the correlation between these assets is -0.43, indicating a moderate, negative linear relationship. And for Figure 1.9(c), GLD returns versus SPY returns, the correlation between these assets is 0.00, indicating no measurable linear relationship between these variables. According to the correlation values for the pairs shown, the strongest linear relationship is between SPY and QQQ because the magnitude of the correlation coefficient is largest.

The correlation coefficient plays a huge role in portfolio construction, particularly from a risk management perspective. Correlation quantifies the relationship between the directional tendencies of two assets. If portfolio assets have highly correlated returns (either positively or negatively), the portfolio is highly exposed to directional risk. To understand how correlation impacts risk, consider the additive property of variance. For two random variables X, Y with individual variances $Var(X), Var(Y)$ and covariance $Cov(X, Y)$, the *combined* variance is given by the following:

$$Var(X + Y) = Var(X) + Var(Y) + 2Cov(X, Y) \tag{1.21}$$

When combining two assets, the overall impact on the uncertainty of the portfolio depends on the uncertainties of the individual assets as well as the covariance between them. Therefore, for every new position that occupies additional portfolio capital, the covariance will increase portfolio uncertainty (high correlation), have little effect on portfolio uncertainty (correlation near zero), or reduce portfolio uncertainty (negative correlation).

Additional Measures of Risk

This chapter has introduced several measures for risk including historical volatility, implied volatility, and the option Greeks. Two additional metrics are worth noting and will appear throughout this text: beta (β) and conditional value at risk (CVaR). Beta is a measure of systematic risk and specifically quantifies the volatility of the stock relative to that of the overall market, which is typically estimated with a reference asset, such as SPY. Given the market's returns, R_m, a stock with returns R_i has the following beta:

$$\beta = \frac{\text{Cov}(R_i, R_m)}{\text{Var}(R_m)} \qquad (1.22)$$

The volatility of a stock relative to the market can then be evaluated according to the following:

- $\beta > 1$: The asset tends to move more than the market. (For example, if the beta of a stock is 1.5, then the asset will tend to move $1.50 for every $1 the market moves.)
- $\beta = 1$: The asset movements tend to match those of the market.
- $0 < \beta < 1$: The asset is less volatile than the market. (For example, if the beta of a stock is 0.5, then the asset will be 50% less volatile than the market.)
- $\beta = 0$: The asset has no systematic risk (market risk).
- $\beta < 0$: The asset tends to move inversely to the market as a whole.

This metric is essential for portfolio management, where it is used in the formulation of beta-weighted delta. This will be covered in more detail in Chapter 7.

Value at risk (VaR) is another distribution statistic that is especially useful when dealing with heavily skewed distributions. VaR is an estimate of the potential losses for a portfolio or position over a given time frame at a specific likelihood level based on historical behavior. For example, a position with a daily VaR of –$100 at the 5% likelihood level can expect to lose $100 (or more) in a single day at most 5% of the time. This means that the bottom 5% of occurrences on the historical daily P/L distribution are –$100 or worse. For a visualization, see the historical daily returns distribution for SPY in Figure 1.10.

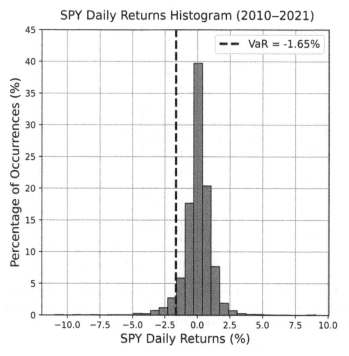

Figure 1.10 SPY daily returns distribution from 2010–2021. Included is the VaR at the 5% likelihood level, indicating that SPY lost at most 1.65% of its value on 95% of all days.

For strategies with significant negative tail skew, VaR gives a numerical estimate for the extreme loss potential according to past tendencies. To place more emphasis on the negative tail of a distribution and determine a more extreme loss estimate, traders may use CVaR, otherwise known as expected shortfall. CVaR is an estimate for the expected loss of portfolio or position if the extreme loss threshold (VaR) is crossed. This is calculated by taking the average of the distribution losses past the VaR benchmark. To see how VaR and CVaR compare for SPY returns, refer to Figure 1.11.

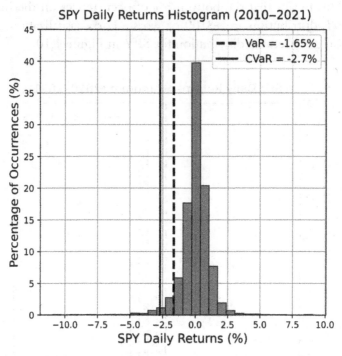

Figure 1.11 SPY daily returns distribution from 2010–2021. Included are VaR and CVaR at the 5% likelihood level. A CVaR of 2.7% indicates that SPY can expect an average daily loss of roughly 2.7% on the worst 5% of days.

The choice between using VaR and CVaR depends on the risk profile of the portfolio or position considered. CVaR is more sensitive to tail losses and provides a metric that is more conservative from the perspective of risk, which is more suitable for the kind of instruments focused on in this book.

Chapter 2

The Nature of Volatility Trading and Implied Volatility

Traders often hedge against periods of extreme market volatility (either to the upside or the downside) using options. Options are effectively financial insurance, and they are priced according to similar principles as other forms of insurance. Premiums increase or decrease according to the *perceived* risk of a given underlying (a result of supply and demand for those contracts), just as the cost of hurricane insurance increases or decreases depending on the perceived risk of hurricanes in a given area. To quantify the perceived risk in the market, traders use implied volatility (IV).

Implied volatility is the value of volatility that would make the current market price for an option be the fair price for that option in a given model, such as Black-Scholes.[1] When options prices *increase* (i.e., there is more demand for insurance), IV increases accordingly, and when options prices decrease, IV decreases. IV is, thus, a proxy for the *sentiment* of market risk as it relates to supply and demand for financial insurance. IV gives the perceived *magnitude* of expected price movements; it is not directional.[2] Table 2.1 gives a numerical example.

Table 2.1 Two underlyings with the same price and put contracts on each underlying with identical parameters (number of shares, put strike, contract duration). The contract prices differ, indicating that these two instruments have different implied volatilities.

45-day Put Contract	Underlying A	Underlying B
Underlying Price	$101	$101
Strike Price	$100	$100
Contract Price	$10	$5

The price of the put is around 10% of the stock price for underlying A and 5% of the stock price for underlying B. This suggests that there is more perceived uncertainty associated with the price of underlying A compared to underlying B. Equivalently, this indicates that the anticipated magnitude of future moves in the underlying price is larger for underlying A compared to underlying B.

Demand for options tends to increase when the historical volatility of an underlying increases unexpectedly, particularly with large moves to the downside. This means that IV tends to be positively correlated with historical volatility and negatively correlated with price. However, there are exceptions to this rule, as IV is based on the perceived risk and not on historical risk directly. IV may increase due to factors that are not directly

---

[1] Implied volatility (IV), like historical volatility, is a percentage and pertains to log returns. It is common to represent IV as either a decimal (0.X) or percentage (X%). An IV index, which is an instrument that tracks IV and will be introduced later in this chapter, is typically represented using points (X) but should be understood as a percentage (X%).

[2] It is possible to get directional expected move information about an underlying by analyzing the IV across various strikes. This will be elaborated on more in the appendix.

related to price movements, such as company-specific uncertainty (earnings reports, silly tweets from the CEO) or larger-scale macroeconomic uncertainty (political conflict, proposed legislative measures). This also means that volatility profiles vary significantly from instrument to instrument, which will be discussed more later in the chapter.

Similar to historical volatility, IV gives a one standard deviation range of annual returns for an instrument. Though historical volatility represents the realized *past volatility of returns*, IV is the approximation for *future volatility of returns* because it is based on how the market is using options to hedge against future price changes. While each option for an underlying has its own implied volatility, the "overall" IV of an asset is normally calculated from 30-day options and is a rough annualized volatility forecast.[3]

> Example: An asset has a price of $100 and an IV of 0.10 (10%). Therefore, the asset is expected to move about 10% to the upside or the downside by the end of the following year. This means the ending price will most likely be between $90 and $110.

The volatility forecast can also be scaled to approximate the expected price across days, weeks, months, or longer. The equations used to calculate the expected price ranges of an asset over some forecasting period are given below.[4]

$$1\sigma \text{ expected range (\%)} = \text{IV} \cdot \sqrt{\frac{\text{No. of Calendar Days}}{365}} \qquad (2.1)$$

---

[3] IV yields a rough approximation for the expected price range, but this is not how the expected range is typically calculated on most trading platforms. Refer to the appendix for more information about how expected range is calculated more precisely. For the time being, we are using this simplified formula since it is most intuitive.

[4] When ignoring the risk-free rate, the expected price range over T days for a stock with price S and volatility σ can be estimated by $Se^{\pm\sigma\sqrt{T/365}}$. The formula in Equation (2.2) is an approximation because, for small x values, $e^x \approx 1 + x$. This approximation becomes less valid when x is large, meaning this expected range calculation is less accurate when IV is high. This will be explored more in the appendix.

$$1\sigma \text{ expected range (\$)} = \text{Stock price} \cdot \text{IV} \cdot \sqrt{\frac{\text{No. of Calendar Days}}{365}}$$

$$(2.2)$$

These estimates of expected range will be used to formulate options strategies in future chapters. The time frame for the expected range is often scaled to match the contract duration. Most examples in this book will have a duration of 45 days to expiration (DTE) (or 33 trading days), so implied volatilities are typically multiplied by 0.35 to ensure forecasts match the duration of the contract.

The expected move cone is helpful to visualize this likely price range for an instrument according to market speculation. The width of the cone is calculated using Equation (2.2) and scales with the IV of the underlying. More specifically, the cones are wider in higher volatility environments and narrower when volatility is low and the expected range is tighter. Consider the expected move cones shown in Figure 2.1, corresponding to the expected price ranges for SPY.

Figure 2.1(c) shows the realized price trajectory for SPY in December 2019, which stayed within its expected price range for the majority of the 45-day duration. Prices tend to stay within their expected range more often than not, and the assumptions of the Black-Scholes model can be used to develop a theoretical estimate for how often that should be.

Trading Volatility

An inconceivable number of factors affect prices in financial markets, which makes precisely forecasting price movements extremely difficult. Arguably, the most reliable way to form expectations around future price trends is using statistics from past price data and financial models. IV is derived from current options prices and the Black-Scholes options pricing model, meaning that the Black-Scholes assumptions can be used to add statistical context to the expected price range. More specifically, one can infer the likelihood of a stock price remaining within its IV-derived price range because stock returns are assumed to be normally distributed. The one standard deviation range of the normal distribution encompasses 68.2% of event outcomes, so there is theoretically a 68.2% chance the price of an equity lands within its expected range. This probability can also be generalized over any timescale using Equation (2.1).

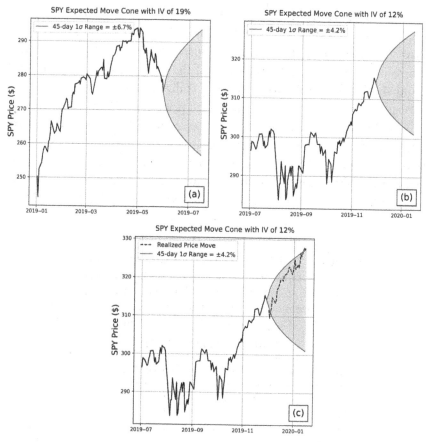

Figure 2.1 (a) The 45-day expected move cone for SPY in early 2019. The price of SPY was roughly $275, and the IV was around 19%, corresponding to a 45-day expected price range of ±6.7% (Equation (2.1)) or ±$18 (Equation (2.2)). (b) The 45-day expected move cone for SPY when IV was 12%. (c) The same expected move cone as (b) with the realized price over 45 days.

Example: An asset has a price of $100 and an IV of 0.10 (10%). The asset price is expected to remain between $90 and $110 by the end of the following year with 68% certainty. Equivalently, the asset price is expected to remain between $96 and $104 58 days from today with 68% certainty (calculated using Equation (2.2)).

However, historical data show that perceived uncertainty in the market (IV) tends to overstate the realized underlying price move more often than theory suggests. Though theory predicts that IV should overstate the realized move roughly only 68% of the time, market IV (estimated using the IV for SPY) overstated the realized move 87% of the time between 2016 and 2021. This means the price for SPY stayed within its expected price range more often than estimated. Realized moves were larger just 13% of the time, indicating that IV rarely understates the realized risk in the market. The *exact* degree to which IV tends to overstate realized volatility depends on the instrument. For example, consider the IV overstatement rates of the stocks and exchange-traded funds (ETFs) in Table 2.2.

Table 2.2   IV overstatement of realized moves for six assets from 2016–2021. Assets include SPY (S&P 500 ETF), GLD (gold commodity ETF), SLV (silver commodity ETF), AAPL (Apple stock), GOOGL (Google stock), AMZN (Amazon stock).

Volatility Data (2016–2021)

Asset	IV Overstatement Rate
SPY	87%
GLD	79%
SLV	89%
AAPL	70%
GOOGL	79%
AMZN	77%

Different assets are more or less prone to stay within their expected move range depending on their unique risk profile. Stocks are subject to single-company risk factors and tend to be more volatile. ETFs, which contain a variety of assets, are inherently diversified and tend to be less prone to dramatic price swings. For example, the S&P 500 includes Apple, but it also includes around 499 other companies. This means that a tech-sector specific event will have a bigger impact on APPL compared to SPY. Commodities like gold and silver also tend to be less volatile than individual stocks, meaning they are less prone to spikes in IV and have more predictable returns. Although the IV overstatement rates differ between instruments, one can conclude that *fear* of large price moves is usually greater than realized price moves in the market. So, how exactly can options traders capitalize on this knowledge of IV and IV overstatement?

Let's revisit the example of hurricane insurance. The price for hurricane insurance is proportional to the expected cost of potential hurricane damage in the area. These prices are based on historical hurricane activity and forecasts of future events, which may underestimate, overestimate, or match the realized outcomes. People who *sell* hurricane insurance initially collect premiums, with the value depending on the perceived risk of home damage. During uneventful hurricane seasons, most policies go unused, and insurers keep the majority of premiums initially collected. In the unlikely event that hurricane damage is *significantly* worse than expected in an area dense with policyholders, insurers take very large losses. Insurance companies essentially make small, consistent profits the majority of the time while being exposed to large, infrequent losses.

Financial insurance carries a similar risk-reward trade-off as sellers make small, consistent profits most of the time but run the risk of large losses in extreme circumstances. IV yields an approximate price range forecast for a given underlying with 68% certainty. This means there is a 68% chance that the calls with strikes at the upper end of the expected range and puts with strikes at the lower end will both expire with no intrinsic value. For example, if traders sold one call and one put with strikes along the expected move cone, they would theoretically profit with 68% certainty. If the underlying price were to move unexpectedly to the upside or the downside, however, the traders may take substantial losses.

Unlike sellers of hurricane insurance, options sellers have more room to strategize and more control over their risk-reward profile. Premium sellers can choose when to sell insurance and how to construct contracts most likely to be profitable. Because IV is a proxy for the demand for options and the inflation of premium, it can be used to identify opportune times to sell insurance. Additionally, because IV can be used to estimate the most likely price range for a specific asset, premium sellers can use IV to structure those positions so they likely expire worthless, like in the previous example. Options sellers (or short premium traders) have the long-term statistical advantage over options buyers, with the trade-off of exposure to unlikely, potentially significant losses. Because of that long-term statistical advantage, short premium trading is the focus of this book, with the next chapter detailing the mechanics of trading based on implied volatility.

The States of VIX

SPY is frequently used as a proxy for the broader market. It is also a baseline underlying for the short options strategies in this book because it is highly diversified across market sectors and has minimal idiosyncratic risk factors. The CBOE Volatility Index (VIX) is meant to track the annualized IV for SPY and is derived from 30-day index options. As SPY is a proxy for the broader market, the VIX, therefore, gauges the perceived risk of the broader market. For context, from 1990 to 2021, the VIX ranged from roughly 10 to a peak of just over 80 in March 2020 during the COVID-19 pandemic.[5]

Unlike equities, whose prices typically drift from their starting values over time, IV tends to revert back to a long-term value following a cyclic trend. This is because equities are used to estimate the perceived value of a company, sector, or commodity, but IV tracks the uncertainty sentiment of the market, which can only stay elevated for so long. During typical bull market conditions, the VIX hovers at a relatively low value at or below its average of 18.5. This is known as a lull state. When market uncertainty rapidly increases for whatever reason, often in response to large sudden price changes, the VIX expands and spikes far above its steady-state value. Once the market adjusts to the new volatility conditions or the volatile conditions dissipate, the VIX gradually contracts back to a lull state. To see an example of this cycle, refer to Figure 2.2.

---

[5] Note that volatility indices, such as the VIX, will be represented using points but are meant to be understood as a percentage. For example, a VIX of 30 corresponds to an annualized implied volatility of 30%.

SPY IV

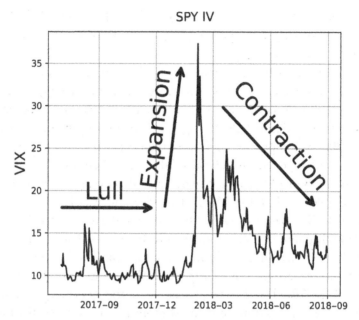

Figure 2.2 The three phases of the VIX, using data from early 2017 to late 2018.

When comparing how often the VIX is in each state, one finds the following approximate rates:

- Lull (70%): IV consistently remains below or near its long-term average. This state occurs when market prices trend upward gradually and market uncertainty is consistently low.
- Expansion (10%): IV expansion usually follows a prolonged lull period and is marked by expanding market uncertainty and typically large price moves in the underlying equity.
- Contraction (20%): IV contraction follows an expansion and is marked by a continued decline in IV. A contraction turns into a lull when IV reverts back to its long-term average.

Lull periods are most common and tend to be much longer than the average expansion or contraction period. Since 2000, the average lull period was more than three times the length of the average expansion or contraction. When expansions do happen, the higher the IV peak, the faster the VIX contracts. For example, according to data from 2005 to 2020, when the VIX contracted from 20 to 16 points (20% decrease), it took an average of 75.3 trading days to do so. However, when the VIX contracted from 70 to 56 points (also a 20% decrease), it only took an average of four trading days.

Spikes in the VIX are generally caused by unprecedented market or worldwide events. For example, the VIX reached over 80 in November 2008 during the peak of the worldwide financial crisis and hit its all-time high of 82.69 in March 2020 during the COVID-19 pandemic. The VIX peak of 2020 was especially unprecedented as the first major spike due to COVID-19 happened on February 28, 2020 when the VIX hit 40.11. This VIX high in 2020 had not been reached since February 2018, and it followed a 96-day lull. On March 16, 2020, the VIX hit 82.69, making the 2020 VIX expansion one of the most rapid ever recorded.

Though contraction periods tend to be longer than expansions but much shorter than lulls, fairly long contractions tend to follow major sell-offs or corrections. For example, the VIX contraction following the 2008 sell-off lasted well over a year, and the contraction following the 2020 sell-off lasted more than 10 months. This is normally because it takes time for the market (and specific subsectors) to revert to regular conditions following such broad macroeconomic shocks.

Premium sellers can potentially profit in any type of market, whether it be during volatility expansions (bearish), contractions (bullish/neutral), or lulls (neutral) if adopting an appropriate strategy for the volatility conditions. Generally, the most favorable trading state for selling premium is when IV contracts. This is because IV contracts when premium prices deflate, meaning that options traders who sold positions in high IV[6] are able to buy identical positions back in low IV at a lower price, thus profiting from the difference. Volatility expansions, on the other hand, have the potential to generate significant losses for short premium traders.

Volatility expansions tend to occur when there are large movements in the underlying price and uncertainty increases, causing options on that underlying to become more expensive. If traders sell premium during

---

[6] It's important to note that the threshold for high IV is different for every asset because each instrument is subject to unique risk factors. Evaluating IV can be difficult because there is so much variability between assets, but there will be a more in-depth discussion of this in the following chapter.

an expansion period once IV is *already elevated*, then the traders can capitalize on higher premium prices and the increased likelihood of a volatility contraction. However, if traders sell premium during a lull period, when the expected range is tight, and volatility *transitions* into an expansion period, then those traders will likely take large losses from the underlying price moving far outside the expected range. Additionally, to close their positions early, traders must buy back their options for more than they received in initial credit and incur a loss from the difference.

Short premium traders can profit in any type of market, but the risk of significant losses for short premium traders is highest when volatility is *low*. Unexpected transitions from a volatility lull to an expansion do not happen often, but when they do happen, they can be detrimental to an account. It is still necessary to trade during these low-IV periods because IV spends the majority of the time in this state, but risk management during this period is crucial. These risk management techniques will be outlined in the upcoming chapters.

This cyclic trend (lull, expansion, contraction, lull) is easily observable when looking at a relatively stable volatility index, such as the VIX. However, this trend, which we will describe as IV reversion, is present in some capacity for *all* IV signals.

IV Reversion

Certain types of signals tend to revert back to a long-term value following a significant divergence. Although this concept cannot be empirically proven or disproven, the reversion of IV is a core assumption in options trading.[7] The reversion dynamics and the minimum IV level vary across instruments, but reversion is assumed to be present in *all* IV signals to some extent. To understand this, first consider the probability of large magnitude returns for four assets with different risk profiles: SPY, GLD, AAPL, and AMZN. A comparison of these probabilities is shown in Table 2.3.

---

[7] The value that the signal reverts back to is roughly the long-term mode of the distribution, or the volatility that has occurred most often historically.

Table 2.3   Rates thats different assets experienced daily returns larger than 1%, 3%, and 5% in magnitude. For example, there is a 22% chance that SPY returns more than 1% or less than −1% in a single day (according to past data).

Probability of Surpassing Daily Returns Magnitude (2015–2021)

Asset	> 1% Magnitude	> 3% Magnitude	> 5% Magnitude
SPY	22%	3%	0.8%
GLD	19%	1%	0.1%
AAPL	43%	9%	2%
AMZN	45%	10%	3%

Compared to assets like SPY and GLD, AMZN and AAPL are more volatile. These tech stocks experience large daily returns roughly three times as often as SPY and roughly 10 times as often as GLD. Each of these assets is subject to unique risk factors, but all are expected to have reverting IV signals nonetheless. Figure 2.3 shows these volatility profiles graphically.

Figure 2.3 demonstrates how IV has tended to revert back to a long-term baseline for each of the different assets, and it also demonstrates that elevated uncertainty is *unsustainable* in financial markets. Events may occur that spark fear in the market and drive up the demand for insurance, but as fear inevitably dissipates and the market adapts to the new conditions, IV deflates back down. This phenomenon has significant implications for short options traders. As stated in Chapter 1, it is controversial whether directional price assumptions are statistically valid or not as trading according to pricing forecasts has never been proven to consistently outperform the market. IV is assumed to eventually revert down following inflations from its stable volatility state unlike asset prices, which drift from their initial value with time. The timescale for these contractions is unpredictable, but this nonetheless indicates some statistical validity to make downward directional assumptions about volatility once it is elevated.

Figure 2.3 also shows how volatility profiles vary greatly across instruments. More volatile assets like Apple and Amazon stocks have higher IV averages, twice that of SPY and gold in this case, and experience expansion events more often. Single-company factors, such as quarterly earnings reports, pending mergers, acquisitions, and

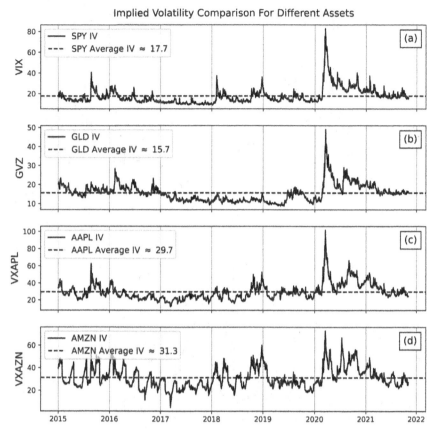

Figure 2.3   IV indexes for different assets with their respective averages (dashed) from 2015–2021. Assets include (a) SPY (S&P 500 ETF), (b) GLD (gold commodity ETF), (c) AAPL (Apple stock), and (d) AMZN (Amazon stock).

executive changes can all cause volatility spikes not seen in diversified assets and portfolios. However, this increased volatility also comes with higher credits and more volatility contraction opportunities for premium sellers.[8] For an example of how the propensity for expansions and contractions differs between stocks with earnings and a diversified ETF, refer to Figures 2.4(a)–(c). Marked are the earnings report dates for each stock or the date when the company reported its quarterly profits (after-tax net income).

---

[8] Such underlyings can be used for earnings plays, which will be discussed in a Chapter 9.

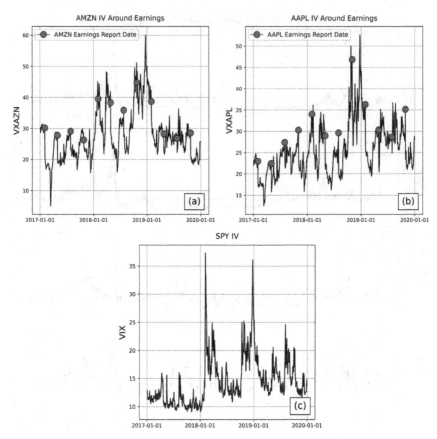

Figure 2.4 Implied volatility indexes for different equities from 2017–2020 with earnings dates marked (if applicable). Assets include (a) AMZN (Amazon stock), (b) AAPL (Apple stock), and (c) SPY (S&P 500 ETF).

With tech stocks like AMZN and AAPL, it's common for IV to increase sharply prior to earnings and contract almost immediately afterward. The previous graphs show that sharp IV expansions happen less frequently with a more diversified market ETF, such as SPY. These figures indicate that when SPY does experience a volatility expansion, it generally takes much longer to contract. From 2017 to 2020, the VIX only rose above 35 two times and, in both situations, took roughly half a month to contract down to its original level. Meanwhile, volatility levels of AMZN and AAPL rose above 40 many times and even had a few spikes above 50, or in the case of AMZN, almost 60.

Takeaways

1. IV is a proxy for the sentiment of market risk derived from supply and demand. When options prices increase, IV increases; when options prices decrease, IV decreases. IV also gives the perceived magnitude of future movement, and it is not directional.

2. Demand for options tends to increase when the historical volatility of an underlying increases unexpectedly, particularly with large moves to the downside. IV tends to be positively correlated with historical volatility and negatively correlated with price, but it is ultimately based on the *perceived* market risk and not directly on price information.

3. IV can be used to estimate the expected price range of an instrument. IV gives a one standard deviation *expected* range because it is based on how the market is using options to hedge against future periods of volatility.

4. Because stock returns are assumed to be normally distributed, theoretically, there is a 68.2% chance the price of an equity lands within its expected range over a given time frame. However, historical data show that prices stay within their expected ranges more often than theoretically estimated. For example, market IV (estimated using the IV for SPY) overstated the realized move 87% of the time between 2016 and 2021.

5. Options sellers have the long-term statistical advantage over options buyers, with the trade-off of exposure to unlikely, potentially significant losses. Because IV is a proxy for the demand for options and the inflation of premium, it can be used to identify opportune times to sell insurance. Premium sellers can also use IV to structure positions so they are likely to expire worthless, the ideal outcome for the short position.

6. Volatility profiles differ significantly between assets, but all IV signals are assumed to revert back to some long-term value following significant diversions. Stated differently, IV tends to contract back to a long-term value following significant expansions from its lull volatility state. This phenomenon indicates that there is some degree of statistical validity when making downward directional assumptions about volatility once it's inflated.

Chapter 3

Trading Short Premium

O ptions are highly versatile instruments. They can be used to hedge the directional risk of a stock, or they can be used as a source of profits. As alluded to in the example of hurricane insurance, short premium positions can be used to generate small, consistent profits for those willing to accept the tail risk. The mechanics of short premium trading are subtle, but many of the core concepts can be introduced in an intuitive way with some simple gambling analogies. For example, when using options for profit generation (i.e., not risk mitigation), the long-term performance of long and short options can be analogized with slot machines.

- **Buying Options for profit** is like playing the slot machines. Gamblers who play enough times may hit the jackpot and receive a huge payout. However, despite the potential payouts, most players average a loss in the long run because they are taking small losses the majority of the time. Investors who buy options are betting on large, often directional moves in the underlying asset. Those assumptions

may be correct and yield significant profits occasionally, but underlying prices ultimately stay within their expected ranges most of the
time. This results in small, frequent losses on unused contracts and
an average loss over time.

- **Selling Options for profit** is like owning the slot machines.
  Casino owners have the long-run statistical advantage for every
  game, an edge particularly high for slots. Owners may occasionally
  pay out large jackpots, but as long as people play enough and the
  payouts are manageable, they are compensated for taking on this risk
  with nearly guaranteed profit in the long term. Similarly, because
  short options carry tail risk but provide small, consistent profits
  from implied volatility (IV) overstatement, then they should average
  a profit in the long run if risk is managed appropriately.

Long premium strategies have a high profit potential but cannot be
consistently timed to ensure profit in the long term. This is because
outlier underlying moves and IV expansions that benefit long premium
positions are strongly linked to external events (such as natural disasters or
political conflict), which are relatively difficult to reliably predict. Short
premium strategies, on the other hand, profit more often and have the
long-term statistical advantage if investors manage risks appropriately.

Similar to the slot machine owner, a short premium trader must
reduce the impact of outlier losses to reach a large number of occurrences (trades) and realize the positive long-term averages. This is most
effectively done by limiting position size and by adjusting portfolio exposure according to current market conditions. This chapter will, therefore,
cover the following broader concepts in volatility trading:

1. Trading in high IV: Identifying favorable conditions for opening
   short premium trades.
2. Number of occurrences: Reaching the minimum number of trades
   required to achieve long-term averages.
3. Portfolio allocation and position sizing: Establishing an appropriate
   level of risk for the given market conditions.
4. Active management and efficient capital allocation: Understanding
   the benefits of managing trades prior to expiration.

IV plays a crucial role in trading short premium. Remember that IV is a measure of the *sentiment* of uncertainty in the market. It is a proxy for the amount of *fear* among premium buyers (or *excitement*, depending on your personality) and a measure of *opportunity* for premium sellers. When market uncertainty increases, premium prices also increase, and premium sellers receive more compensation for being exposed to large losses. However, IV is also instrumental when managing exposure to extreme losses and establishing appropriate position sizes.

Background: A Note on Visualizing Option Risk

When discussing the risk-reward trade-off of trading short premium, it is helpful to contextualize concepts and statistics with respect to a specific strategy. The next few chapters will focus on a *short strangle*, an options strategy consisting of a short out-of-the-money (OTM) call and a short OTM put:

- A short OTM call (the right to buy an asset at a certain price) has a bearish directional assumption. The seller profits when the underlying price stays below the specified strike price.
- A short OTM put (the right to sell an asset at a certain price) has a bullish directional assumption. The seller profits when the underlying price stays above the specified strike price.

These two contracts combine to form a strangle. This is an example of an *undefined risk* strategy, where the loss is theoretically unlimited. The short call has undefined risk because stock prices can increase indefinitely, meaning the potential loss to the upside is unknown. Though short puts technically cannot lose more than 100 times the strike price, this potential loss is large enough that they are also considered undefined risk. Defined risk strategies, where the maximum loss is limited by the construction of the trade, have pros and cons that will be discussed in Chapter 5. For simplicity, the strangle is used to formulate most examples in this book.

Strangles have a neutral directional assumption for the contract seller, meaning it is typically profitable when the price of the underlying stays within the range defined by the short call strike and short put strike. Investors often define the strikes of a strangle according to the expected range of the underlying price (or some multiple of the expected range) over the contract duration. The one standard deviation expected range can be approximated with the current implied volatility of the underlying, as shown in Chapter 2.

Figure 3.1   The price of SPY in the last five months of 2019. Included is the 45-day expected move cone calculated from the IV of SPY in December 2019. The edges of the cones are labeled according to appropriate strikes for an example strangle.

Figure 3.1 shows that SPY was priced at roughly $315 around December 2019, when the current IV for SPY was 12% (corresponding to a VIX level of 12). This means the price for SPY was forecasted to move between −4.2% and +4.2% over the next 45 days with a 68% certainty. This is equivalent to a 45-day forecast of the price of SPY staying between $302 and $328 approximately. A contract with a strike price corresponding to the 1σ expected move range is approximately a 16Δ contract. In this scenario, a 45 days to expiration (DTE) short SPY call with a strike price of $328 is a −16Δ contract roughly, and a 45

DTE short SPY put with a strike price of $302 is approximately a 16Δ contract. The two positions combined form a delta-neutral position known as a 45 DTE 16Δ SPY strangle.[1]

The strangle buyer and seller are making different bets:

- The strangle buyer assumes that SPY's price will move beyond expectation within the next 45 days, either to the upside or the downside. More specifically, the long strangle yields profit if the price of SPY significantly increases above $328 or decreases below $302 prior to expiration.

- The strangle seller profits if the position expires when the underlying price is within or near its expected range or if the position is closed when the contract is trading for a cheaper price than when it was opened (IV contraction).

Because there is a 68% chance the underlying will stay within its expected range, the short position theoretically has a 68% chance of being profitable. However, since the underlying price tends to stay in its expected range more often than theoretically predicted, this results in the probability of profit (POP) of short strangles held to expiration being much higher.

For example, consider the profit and loss (P/L) distributions for the short 45 DTE 16Δ SPY strangle in Figures 3.2(a)–(c). These distributions were generated using historical options data and are useful for visualizing the long-term risk-reward profile and likely trade-by-trade outcomes for this type of contract. Each occurrence in the histogram corresponds to the final P/L of a short strangle held to expiration.[2] P/L can be represented as a raw dollar amount or as a percentage of initial credit (the fraction of option premium that the seller ultimately kept).[3]

---

[1] These are approximate strikes for the 16Δ SPY strangle calculated using the equation from Chapter 2. The actual strikes for a 16Δ SPY strangle are calculated using more complex estimations for expected range, which will be touched on in the appendix.

[2] It is difficult to make a one-to-one comparison between equity returns and option P/Ls because these instruments operate over different timescales. The closest option analog to an equity returns distribution is a distribution for the ending P/Ls of a particular strategy.

[3] Statistics represented as a percentage of initial credit are more representative of long-term values than those represented with dollars. Equity prices drift with time, meaning the prices for their options do as well. Normalizing P/L statistics by the initial credit makes them more robust to changes in time but also makes comparisons between strategies less intuitive. This book will often represent option statistics in dollars, but remember these statistics are averaged over fairly long time frames.

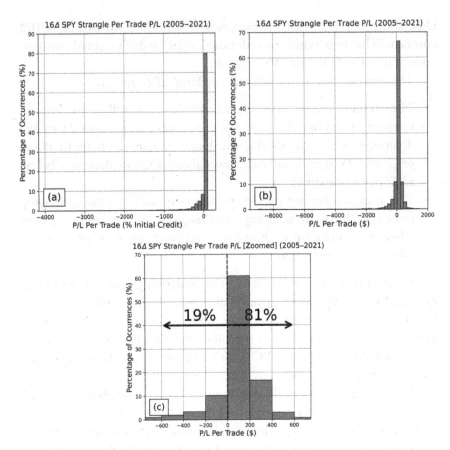

Figure 3.2   (a) Historical P/L distribution (% of initial credit) for short 45 DTE 16Δ SPY strangles, held to expiration from 2005–2021. (b) Historical P/L distribution ($) for short 45 DTE 16Δ SPY strangles, held to expiration from 2005–2021. (c) The same distribution as in (b) but zoomed in near $0. The percentage of occurrences on either side of $0 have been labeled.

Figure 3.2(c) shows that 81% of occurrences are *positive* and only 19% are *negative*. This means this strategy has historically profited 81% of the time and only taken losses 19% of the time, significantly higher than the 68% POP that the simplified theory suggests. Over the long run, this strategy was *profitable* and averaged a P/L of $44 (or 28% of the initial credit) per trade. However, notice the P/L distributions for this strategy are highly skewed and carry significant tail risk. As shown in Figure 3.2(a), these tail losses are unlikely but could potentially amount to −1,000% or even −4,000% of the initial credit. In other words, if a trader receives $100 in initial credit for selling a SPY strangle, there is a slim chance of losing upward of $4,000 on that trade according to historical behavior. This is the trade-off for the high POPs of short premium strategies.

The possibility of outlier losses should not be surprising because placing a short premium trade is betting against large, unexpected price swings. For a relatively stable asset like SPY, these types of swings rarely happen. When they do, things can fly off the handle rapidly, such as during the 2008 recession or 2020 sell-off. Consequently, the most important goals for a short premium trader are to profit consistently enough to cover moderate, more likely losses and to construct a portfolio that can survive those unlikely extreme losses.

Background: A Note on Quantifying Option Risk

Approximating the historical risk of a stock or exchange-traded fund (ETF) is relatively straightforward. Equity log returns distributions are fairly symmetric and resemble a normal distribution, thus justifying that standard deviation of returns (historical volatility) be used to approximate historical risk. However, a short option P/L distribution is highly skewed and subject to substantial outlier risk. Due to this more complex risk profile, using option P/L standard deviation as a lone proxy for risk *significantly* misrepresents the true risk of the strategy. Therefore, the following metrics will be used to more thoroughly discuss the risk of short options: standard deviation of P/L, skew, and conditional value at risk (CVaR).[4]

The standard deviation of P/L encompasses the range that the *majority* of endings P/Ls fall within for a given strategy historically. The standard deviation for financial strategies is commonly interpreted relative to the normal distribution, where one standard deviation accounts for 34% of the distribution on either side of the mean. For options P/L distributions, however, the one standard deviation of P/L typically

---

[4] These are past-looking risk metrics. Metrics of forward-looking risk include implied volatility and buying power reduction (BPR), which will be covered in the following chapter. Forward-looking metrics are the focus of this book and more relevant in applied trading, but past-looking metrics are still included for the sake of completeness and education.

accounts for more than 68% of the total occurrences and the density of occurrences is not symmetric about the mean. Again, consider the P/L distribution for the short 45 DTE 16Δ SPY strangle.

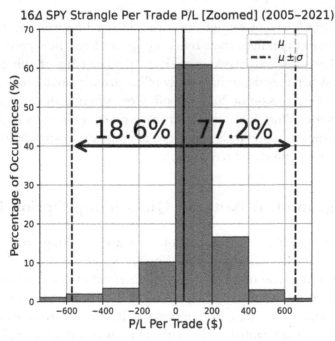

Figure 3.3 Historical P/L distribution ($) for 45 DTE 16Δ SPY strangles, held to expiration from 2005–2021. The distribution has been zoomed in near the mean (solid line), and the percentage of occurrences within ±1σ of the mean has been labeled.

For 45 DTE 16Δ SPY strangles from 2005–2021, the average P/L was $44, and the standard deviation of P/L was $614. As shown in Figure 3.3, the one standard deviation range accounts for nearly 96% of all occurrences, significantly higher than the ±1σ range for the normal distribution. Additionally, because the distribution is highly asymmetric, the P/Ls in the −1σ range are less likely than the P/Ls in the +1σ range. Due to these factors, the interpretation of standard deviation as a measure of risk must be adjusted. Standard deviation *overestimates* the magnitude of the most likely losses (e.g., a $500 loss is unlikely, but the standard deviation range does not clarify that) and does not account negative tail risk. It does yield a range for the *most likely* profits and losses on a trade-by-trade basis for a given strategy. Therefore, traders can generally form more reliable P/L expectations for strategies with a lower P/L standard deviation.

Skew and CVaR are used to estimate the historical tail risk of a strategy. As covered in Chapter 1, skew is a measure of the asymmetry of a distribution. Strategies with a larger magnitude of negative skew in their P/L distribution have more historical outlier loss exposure. CVaR gives an estimate of the potential loss of a position over a given time frame at a specific likelihood level based on historical behavior. CVaR can be used to approximate the magnitude of an expected worst-case loss and contextualize skew. For example, consider the two example short strangles outlined in Table 3.1.

Table 3.1 Two example short strangles. For Strangle A, CVaR estimates losing at least $200 at most 5% of the time. In this example, the time frame for this loss has not been specified, but one may assume the time frame is identical for both strategies.

Risk Factors	Strangle A	Strangle B
Skew	−5.0	−1.0
CVaR (5%)	−$200	−$2,000

Strangle A has a larger magnitude of negative skew, indicating that this strategy is more susceptible to tail risk and outlier losses compared to Strangle B. However, there is 10 times more capital at risk in an extreme loss scenario for Strangle B compared to Strangle A perhaps because the underlying for Strangle B is more expensive. Generally speaking, strategies with less skew are preferable because those strategies are less susceptible to large, unpredictable losses and perform more consistently. However, the optimal trade ultimately depends on the acceptable amount of per-trade capital at risk according to the trader's personal preferences.

Also note it is difficult to accurately model outlier loss events because they happen rarely. P/L distributions can give an *idea* of the magnitude of extreme losses, but these statistics are averaged over a broad range of market conditions and volatility environments. They are not necessarily representative of outlier risk at the present time. Buying power reduction (BPR), which will be covered in the next chapter, yields an estimate for the worst-case loss of a trade according to current market conditions. Similar to implied volatility, BPR is a forward-looking metric designed to encompass the most likely scope of losses for an undefined risk position.

Trading in High IV

Selling premium once IV is elevated comes with several advantages. Before that discussion, there are subtleties to note when evaluating "how high" the IV of an asset is. Contextualizing the current IV for an asset like SPY is somewhat straightforward because it has a well-known and widely available IV index. The VIX has historically ranged from approximately 10 to 90, has an average of roughly 18, is typically below 20, and rarely surpasses 40. Therefore, a trader can intuitively interpret a level of 15 as fairly low and a level of 35 as fairly high relative to the long-term behavior of the VIX. But how do traders contextualize the current IV relative to a shorter timescale, such as the last year? And how do traders contextualize the current IV for a less popular IV index with a totally different risk profile? For example, is 35 high for VXAZN, the IV index for AMZN?

One way to gauge the degree of IV elevation with respect to some timescale is by converting raw implied volatility into a relative measure such as IV percentile (IVP). IVP is the percentage of days in the past year where the IV was *below* the current IV level, calculated with the following equation. Note that 252 is the number of trading days in a year.

$$IVP = \frac{\text{Number of days in past year with IV below current IV}}{252} \tag{3.1}$$

IVP ranges from 0% to 100%, with a higher number indicating a higher relative IV. This metric normalizes raw IV to put the current level in context, and unlike raw IV, it is comparable between assets. For example, consider the raw IV indexes and the corresponding IVP values for SPY and AMZN shown in Figure 3.4.

IV Index and IV Percentile Comparison (2015–2016)

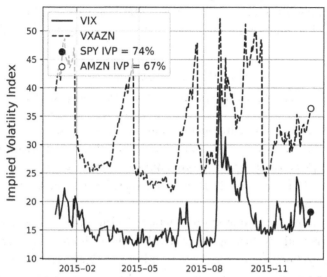

Figure 3.4 The VIX (solid) and VXAZN (dashed) from 2015–2016. Labeled are the IVP values for each index at the end of 2015. When the VIX was roughly 18 SPY had an IVP of 74%, and VXAZN was roughly 36 AMZN had an IVP of 67%.

At the end of 2015, the VIX was near its long-term average of 18 and would have been considered low. However, market IV was below average for the majority of 2015, and a VIX level of 18 was higher than nearly 74% of occurrences from the previous year. A SPY IVP of 74% indicates that IV is fairly elevated relative to the recent market conditions, suggesting that volatility may contract following this expansion period. Comparatively, the volatility index for AMZN at the end of 2015 was 37. This is significantly higher than the VIX at the time but is actually *less elevated* relative to its volatility history from the past year according to the AMZN IVP of 67%. SPY and AMZN have dramatically different volatility profiles, with VXAZN frequently exceeding 35 and the VIX rarely doing so. This makes raw IV a poor metric for comparing relative volatility and a metric like IVP necessary.

Another commonly used relative volatility metric is IV rank (IVR), which compares the current IV level to the historical implied volatility range for that underlying. It is calculated according to the following formula:

$$IVR = \frac{\text{Current IV} - \text{Min. IV over past year}}{\text{Max. IV over past year} - \text{Min. IV over past year}} \quad (3.2)$$

Similar to IVP, IVR normalizes raw IV on a 0% to 100% scale and is comparable between assets. IVR gives a better direct metric for evaluating the price of an option compared to IVP. However, IVP is more robust than IVR because IVR is more sensitive to outlier moves and prone to skew.

Both metrics are suitable for practical decision making because they assist traders with evaluating current volatility levels and selecting a suitable strategy/underlying for those conditions. They are also useful for identifying suitable, high IV underlyings for a portfolio because most assets do not have well-known volatility indices. However, both metrics are fairly unstable, sensitive to timescale, and can be skewed by prolonged outlier events such as sell-offs. Raw IV, assuming that the characteristics of the volatility profile are well understood, is generally a more stable and reliable metric for analyzing long-term trends. Because most studies throughout this book use SPY as a baseline underlying and span several years, raw IV will be used rather than a relative metric.

As previously mentioned, trading short premium when IV is elevated comes with the added benefits of higher credits and more profit potential for sellers. This is shown in Figure 3.5, which includes average credits for 16Δ SPY strangles from 2010–2020 in different volatility environments.

Trading short premium in elevated IV is an effective way to capitalize on higher premium prices and the increased likelihood of a significant volatility contraction. Trading when credits are higher also means common losses tend to be larger (as a dollar amount), but the exposure to outlier risk actually tends to be *lower* when IV is elevated compared to when it's closer to equilibrium. This may seem counterintuitive: If market uncertainty is elevated and there is higher perceived risk, wouldn't short premium strategies carry more outlier risk? Although moves in the underlying tend to be more dramatic when IV is high, the expected range adjusts to account for the new volatility almost immediately, which in many cases reduces the risk of an outlier loss. To understand this,

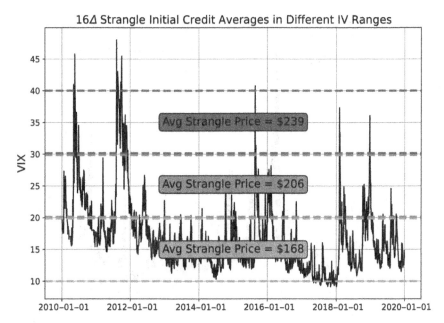

Figure 3.5 SPY IV from 2010–2020. The average prices for 45 DTE 16Δ SPY strangles are labeled at different VIX levels: 10–20, 20–30, and 30–40. When the VIX was between 30 and 40, the average initial credit per one lot for the 16Δ SPY strangle was roughly 42% higher than when the VIX was between 10 and 20.

consider Figures 3.6(a) and (b), showing extreme losses for 16Δ SPY strangles from 2005–2021, with an emphasis on the 2008 recession.

A short 16Δ SPY strangle rarely incurs a loss over $1,000. From 2005–2021, this occurred less than 1% of the time. However, *84% of* these losses occurred when the VIX was below 25. During the initial IV expansion of the 2008 recession (late August to early October), strangles incurred these large losses approximately 56% of the time. Notice in Figure 3.6 that these extreme losses were confined to the initial IV expansion (when the VIX increased from roughly 20 to 35). This is because the market was not anticipating the large downside moves of the recession, as reflected by the VIX being near its long-term average of 18. Because these large swings happened when the expected move range was tight, the historical volatility of the market well exceeded its expected range, and long strangles were highly profitable. Once market uncertainty adjusted to the new conditions and initial credits and expected ranges increased to reflect the perceived risks, the outlier losses for short strangles diminished.

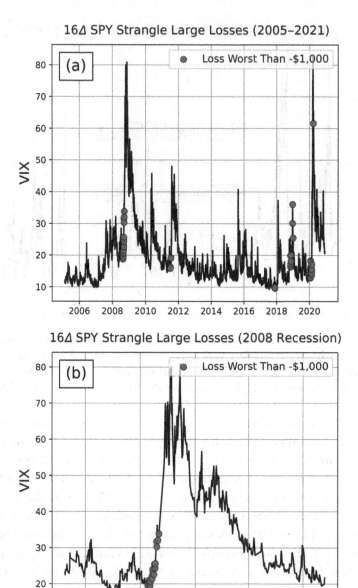

Figure 3.6 (a) SPY IV from 2005–2021. Labeled are the extreme losses for 45 DTE 16Δ SPY strangles held to expiration, meaning losses that are worse than $1,000. (b) The same figure as shown in (a) but zoomed in to 2008–2010, during the 2008 recession.

These unexpected periods of high market volatility are the primary source of extreme loss for short premium positions. These events typically happen when there are large price swings in the underlying and the expected move range is tight (low IV). These extreme expansion events are rare, and trading short premium once IV is elevated tends to reduce this type of exposure. Another way to demonstrate this concept is to consider the amount of skew in the P/L distribution of the 16Δ SPY strangle at different IV levels.

Figures 3.7(a)–(d) illustrate that strangle P/L distributions have less negative skew and smaller tail losses as IV increases. This means that,

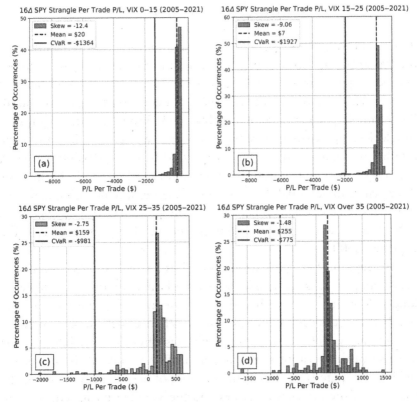

Figure 3.7 Historical P/L distributions for 45 DTE 16Δ SPY strangles, held to expiration from 2005–2021: (a) Occurrences when the VIX is between 0 and 15 (1,603 occurrences total), (b) Occurrences when the VIX is between 15 and 25 (1,506 occurrences total). (c) Occurrences when the VIX is between 25 and 35 (416 occurrences total). (d) Occurrences when the VIX is above 35 (228 occurrences total).

historically, the exposure to negative tail risk was much higher when the VIX was closer to the lower end of its range compared to when the VIX already expanded. The P/L distribution becomes more symmetric as IV increases, indicated by the decreasing magnitude of negative skew. This means that higher IV conditions facilitate more dependable profit and loss expectations than lower IV conditions. As an important note, observe that there are significantly fewer occurrences when the VIX was over 35 (a few hundred occurrences) compared to when the VIX was between 0 and 25 (thousands of occurrences). This brings us to the next point to consider: How often should one trade?

Number of Occurrences

Table games at a casino typically have maximum bet sizes. The house has the statistical edge for every game in the casino, but the house will not necessarily profit from that edge unless patrons bet *often*. In blackjack, the house has an edge of 0.5% if the player's strategy is statistically optimized. So, if gamblers wager $100,000 on blackjack throughout the night, they should lose approximately $500 to the house after a sufficiently large number of hands. If the opponent plays 10 hands at $10,000 per hand, they may win eight hands, three hands, or even all 10 hands. In this case, the variance of potential outcomes is fairly large, and the casino may have to pay fairly large payouts. However, if the opponent plays 1,000 hands at $100 per hand, it is more likely the player's loss will amount to the expected $500.

By capping bet sizes, the casino aims to increase the number of occurrences from a single gambler so the house is more likely to reach long-run averages for each game, a consequence of the law of large numbers and the central limit theorem. When a *small* number of events is randomly sampled from a probability distribution repeatedly and the averages of those samples are compared, the variance of those averages tends to be quite large. But as the number of occurrences increases, the variance of the averages decreases and the sampled means converge to the expected value of the distribution.[5]

---

[5] Specifically, the standard deviation of the average of n independent occurrences is $\frac{1}{\sqrt{n}}$ times the standard deviation of a single occurrence.

Just as the casino aims to realize the long-term edge of table games by capping bet sizes and increasing the number of plays, short premium traders should make many small trades to maximize their chances of realizing the positive long-run expected averages of short premium strategies. For an example of why this is crucial, refer again to the P/L distribution of the 16Δ SPY strangle.

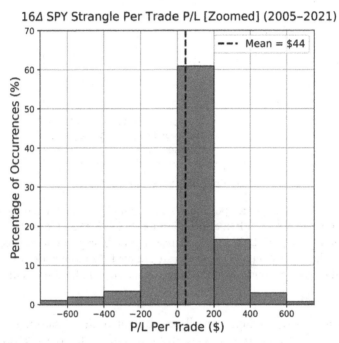

Figure 3.8 Historical P/L distribution for 45 DTE 16Δ SPY strangles, held to expiration from 2005–2021. The dotted line is the long-term average P/L of this strategy.

This strategy, shown in Figure 3.8, has an average P/L per trade of roughly $44 and a POP of 81%. However, these long-term averages were calculated using roughly 3,750 trades. Calculating averages with a large pool of data provides the least amount of statistical error but does not model the occurrences retail traders can realistically achieve. What P/L would short premium traders have averaged if they only placed 10 trades from 2005 to 2021? 100 trades? 500 trades? Figure 3.9 shows a plot of average P/Ls for a collection of sample portfolios, each with a different number of trades randomly selected from the P/L distribution of the 16Δ SPY strangle.

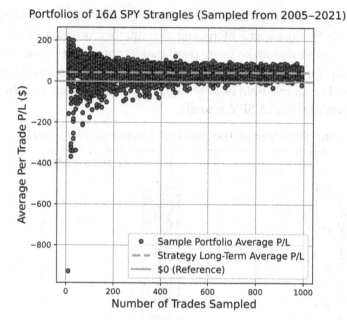

Figure 3.9 P/L averages for portfolios with *N* number of trades, randomly sampled from the historical P/L distribution for 45 DTE 16Δ SPY strangles, held to expiration from 2005–2021. The variance among these portfolio averages is very large when a small number of trades are sampled. As more trades are sampled, the averages converge to the long-term average P/L of this strategy.

As you can see, when a small number of trades is sampled, 10 for example, the average P/L ranges from roughly –$900 to $200. This means that if two traders randomly traded 10 short strangles from 2005 to 2021, one trader may have profited by $2,000, and the other may have lost $9,000. As the number of occurrences increases, the variance of P/L averages among these sample portfolios decreases, and the averages converge toward the long-run expected value of this strategy. In other words, if two traders randomly traded 1,000 short strangles from 2005 to 2021, it would be fairly likely for both to average a P/L near $44 per trade, the historical long-term average P/L of this strategy.

Number of occurrences is a critical factor in achieving long-term averages, and the minimum number of occurrences needed varies with the specific strategy's standard deviation of P/L. For practical purposes, a minimum of roughly 200 occurrences is necessary to reach long-run averages, and more is better. This puts short premium traders in a bit of a predicament because, although trading short premium in high IV is ideal, high IV environments are very uncommon as shown in Table 3.2.

Table 3.2 How often the VIX fell in a given range from 2005–2021.

VIX Data (2005–2021)

VIX Range	% of Occurrences
0–15	43%
15–25	40%
25–35	11%
35+	6%

The VIX is at the low end of its range 43% of the time and below 18.5, its long-term average, the majority of the time. From 2005–2021, the VIX was only above 35 roughly 6% of the time, which does not leave much opportunity for trading short premium in very high IV. To optimize the likelihood of reaching the favorable long-term expected values of this strategy, it is clearly necessary to trade in non-ideal, low volatility conditions. The next section covers how to trade in all market conditions while mitigating the outlier risk in low volatility environments, specifically by maintaining small position sizes and limiting the capital exposed to outlier losses.

Portfolio Allocation and Position Sizing

In practice, short premium traders must strike a balance between being exposed to large losses and reaching a sufficient number of occurrences. Trading in high IV tends to carry less exposure to outlier risk compared to trading in low IV, but trading in low IV is still profitable on average. Unlike long stocks, which are only profitable during bullish conditions, short options may be profitable in bullish, bearish, or neutral conditions and spanning all volatility environments. For the 16Δ SPY strangle from 2005–2021, for example, the majority of occurrences were profitable in all IV ranges. (See Table 3.3.)

Table 3.3   The POPs and average P/Ls in different IV ranges for 45 DTE 16Δ SPY strangles, held to expiration from 2005–2021.

16Δ SPY Strangle Data (2005–2021)

VIX Range	POP	Average P/L
0–15	82%	$20
15–25	78%	$7
25–35	86%	$159
35+	89%	$255

By trading short options strategies in all IV environments, profits accumulate more consistently, and the minimum number of occurrences is more achievable. To manage exposure to outlier risk throughout these environments, it's *essential* to keep position sizes small and limit the total amount of portfolio capital allocated to short premium positions, which can be scaled according to the current outlier risk. The percentage of portfolio capital allocated to short premium strategies should generally range from 25% to 50%, with the remaining capital either kept in cash or a low-risk passive investment.[6] This is because allocating less than 25% severely limits upside growth, while allocating more than 50% may not leave enough capital for a portfolio to recover from an outlier loss event. Because the exposure to outlier risk tends to be higher when IV is low, scaling allocation down in low IV protects portfolio capital from the tail exposure of unexpected market volatility. Once IV increases, scaling short premium capital allocation up increases the potential to profit from higher credits, larger profits, and reduced outlier risk.

Table 3.4   Guidelines for allocating portfolio capital according to market IV.

VIX Range	Max Portfolio Allocation
0–15	25%
15–20	30%
20–30	35%
30–40	40%
40+	50%

---

[6] More specifically, the portfolio capital being referred to here is the portfolio buying power, which we will introduce in the following chapter.

A portfolio should not be overly concentrated in short options strategies for the given market conditions, and the capital allocated to short premium should *also* not be overly concentrated in a single position. An appropriately sized position should not occupy more than 5% to 7% of portfolio capital. The exact percentage varies depending on the POP of the strategies used, and this will be covered in more detail in Chapter 8.

To understand why it's crucial to limit capital exposure and beneficial to scale portfolio allocation according to IV, look at a worst-case scenario: the 2020 sell-off. The 2020 sell-off produced historic losses for short premium positions. From late February to late March 2020, the price of SPY crashed by roughly 34%. For 45 DTE 16Δ SPY strangles, the most extreme losses recorded for this position occurred throughout this time. A 16Δ SPY strangle opening on February 14, 2020, and expiring on March 20, 2020, had a P/L per one lot of roughly –$8,974, the worst recorded loss in 16 years for this type of contract. If traders allocated different percentages of a $100,000 portfolio to short SPY strangles beginning with this worst-case loss, how would those portfolios perform in regular market conditions compared to highly volatile conditions like the 2020 sell-off? Compare three portfolio allocation strategies: allocation by IV guidelines (25–50%), a more conservative allocation (constant 15%), and a more aggressive allocation (constant 65%).[7]

Unsurprisingly, the portfolios perform markedly differently in regular conditions compared to the 2020 sell-off. From 2017 to February of 2020, the aggressive portfolio dramatically outperformed the conservative and IV-allocated portfolios. Throughout this three-year period, the conservative portfolio grew by 13% and the IV-allocated portfolio by 28%, and the aggressive portfolio increased by 78%. Comparatively, from 2017–2020, SPY grew by 50%. This means that a $100,000 portfolio fully allocated to SPY shares would have outperformed

---

[7] This is a highly simplified backtest and should be taken with a grain of salt. These portfolios are highly concentrated in a single position and do not incorporate any complex management strategies. Options are highly sensitive to changes in timescale, meaning that a concurrent portfolio with strangles opened on slightly different days, closed on slightly different days, or with slightly different durations may have performed quite differently than the ones shown here. These backtests show one specific outcome and serve to compare the risk of different allocation percentages in a one-to-one fashion.

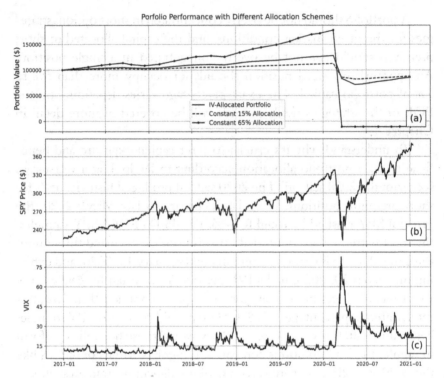

Figure 3.10 (a) Performances from 2017 to 2021, through the 2020 sell-off. Each portfolio has different amounts of capital allocated to approximately 45 DTE 16Δ SPY strangles that are closed at expiration and reopened at the beginning of the expiration cycle. The portfolios are (a) IV-allocated (solid), conservative (dashed), and aggressive (hashed). (b) SPY price from 2017 to 2021. (c) VIX throughout the same time frame.

the conservative and IV-allocated portfolios but underperformed the aggressive portfolio, though it would have required significantly more capital than any of them.

Upon the onset of the highly volatile market conditions of 2020, the highly exposed aggressive portfolio was immediately wiped out. The conservative and IV-allocated portfolios were also impacted by significant losses and declined by 35% and 24%, respectively, from February to March 2020. In all the previous scenarios, each portfolio experienced some degree of loss during the extreme market conditions of the 2020 sell-off. The important thing to note is that portfolios with less capital exposure and position concentration ultimately had the capital to recover following these losses. Following the 2020 sell-off, the conservative portfolio recovered by 7% and the IV-allocated by 20% because this portfolio was able to capitalize on the high IV and higher credits of the sell-off recovery.

For profit goals to be reached *consistently*, it's crucial to construct a portfolio that is robust in every type of market. A highly exposed portfolio takes extraordinary profits in more regular market conditions, but there is a high risk of going under in the rare event of a sell-off or major correction. A more conservative portfolio is well suited for extreme market conditions, but upside profits are limited the majority of the time. Comparatively, scaling capital allocation according to market IV is an effective way to capitalize on higher profits when IV is high, protect capital from outlier losses when IV is low, and achieve reasonable growth with lower capital requirements than purchasing equities directly. More importantly, limiting capital exposure and maintaining appropriate position sizes are arguably the most effective ways to minimize the impact from extreme events. These concepts will be explored in more detail in Chapter 7.

Active Management and Efficient Capital Allocation

Up until now, this book has discussed option risk and profitability for contracts held to expiration. However, short premium traders can also close, or manage, their positions early by purchasing long options with the same underlying, strike, and date of expiration. This can often be profitable as a result of partial theta decay and IV contractions, and it also tends to reduce P/L variability per trade. Options tend to have more P/L fluctuations in the second half of the contract duration compared to the first half, a result of increasing gamma risk. Gamma, as discussed in earlier chapters, is a measure of how sensitive a contract's delta is to changes in the price of the underlying. Gamma increases for near-the-money options as expiration approaches, meaning that delta (and, therefore, the price sensitivity of the option) becomes more unstable in response to moves in the underlying toward the end of the contract.

Managing short positions actively, such as closing a trade prior to expiration and redeploying capital to new positions, is one way to reduce the P/L swings throughout the trade duration, as well as the per-trade loss potential and ending P/L standard deviation. Early management strategies will not necessarily reduce risk in the long term because the cumulative losses of many shorter-term trades may exceed the single loss of a longer-term trade, but they do make per-trade loss potentials more reasonable. This strategy effectively allows traders to assess the viability of a trade before P/L swings become more extreme and assess whether it is an efficient use of portfolio capital to remain in the trade. Compare how the P/Ls of 45 DTE 16Δ SPY strangles are distributed when the contracts are held to expiration versus managed around halfway to expiration (21 DTE).

Table 3.5 Comparison of management strategies for 45 DTE 16Δ SPY strangles from 2005–2021 that are held to expiration and managed early. Statistics include POP, average P/L, standard deviation of P/L, and CVaR at the 5% likelihood level.

16Δ SPY Strangle Statistics (2005–2021)

Statistics	Held to Expiration	Managed at 21 DTE
POP	81%	79%
Average P/L	$44	$30
Average Daily P/L	$1.29	$1.60
Standard Deviation of P/L	$614	$260
CVaR (5%)	−$1,535	−$695

According to the statistics in Table 3.5, strangles managed at 21 DTE carry significantly less negative tail risk and P/L standard deviation on a trade-by-trade basis than strangles held to expiration. Additionally, although early-managed contracts collect less on average per trade, they actually average *more* profit on a daily basis and allow for more occurrences due to the shorter duration.

Managing trades early has several benefits, most of which will be covered in Chapter 6. Much of this decision depends on the acceptable amount of capital to risk on a single trade and whether it is an efficient use of capital to remain in the existing trade. Notice from this example that managed trades take 24 days (21 days remaining on a 45-day duration trade corresponds to an elapsed duration of 24 days) to profit $30 on average and held contracts 45 days to make $44 on average. Trades may accumulate the majority of their profit potential well before expiration, depending on the market and staying in the position for the remainder of the duration may limit upside potential. Closing trades prior to expiration and redeploying capital to a new position in the same underlying is an effective method for increasing the number of occurrences in a given time frame. Redeploying that capital to a position in a different underlying with more favorable characteristics (such as higher IV) can be a more efficient use of capital and can offer elements of risk reduction in certain situations. Taking an active approach to investing and trade management provides more control over portfolio capital allocation and the flexibility to modify trades given new information.

Takeaways

1. Compared to long premium strategies, short premium strategies yield more consistent profits and have the long-term statistical advantage. The trade-off for receiving consistent profits is exposure to large and sometimes undefined losses, which is why the most important goals of a short premium trader are to (1) profit consistently enough to cover moderate and more likely losses and (2) to construct a portfolio that can survive unlikely extreme losses.

2. Unexpected periods of high market volatility are the primary source of extreme loss for short premium positions. These events are highly unlikely but typically happen when large price swings occur in the underlying while the expected move range is tight (low IV). Trading short premium once IV is elevated is one way to consistently reduce this exposure.

3. The profitability of short options strategies depends on having a large number of occurrences to reach positive statistical averages. At minimum, approximately 200 occurrences are needed for the average P/L of a strategy to converge to long-term profit targets and more is better.

4. Although trading short premium in high IV is ideal, high IV environments are somewhat uncommon. This means that short premium traders must strike a balance between being exposed to large losses and reaching a sufficient number of occurrences. Trading short options strategies in all IV environments accumulates profits more

consistently and makes it more likely to reach the minimum number of occurrences. To manage exposure to outlier risk when adopting this strategy, it's essential to maintain small position sizes and limit the amount of capital allocated to short premium positions. This strategy can also be improved by scaling the amount of capital allocated to short premium according to the current market conditions.

5. Managing positions actively is one way to reduce P/L uncertainty on a trade-by-trade basis, use capital more efficiently, and achieve more occurrences in a given time frame. The choice of whether to close a position early and redeploy capital depends on the acceptable amount of capital to risk on a single trade and whether it is an efficient use of capital to remain in the existing trade. These concepts will be explored more in Chapter 6.

Chapter 4

Buying Power Reduction

H aving discussed the nature of implied volatility (IV) and the general risk-reward profile of short premium positions, it's time to introduce some elements of short volatility trading in practice. Because short options are subject to significant tail risk, brokers must reserve a certain amount of capital to cover the potential losses of each position. The capital required to place and maintain a short premium trade is called the buying power reduction (BPR), and the total amount of portfolio capital available for trading is the portfolio buying power.

BPR is the amount of capital required to be set aside in the account to insure a short option position, similar to escrow. BPR is used to evaluate short premium risk on a trade-by-trade basis in two ways:

1. BPR acts as a fairly reliable metric for the worst-case loss for an undefined risk position in current market conditions.
2. BPR is used to determine if a position is appropriate for a portfolio with a certain buying power.

Though BPR is the option counterpart of stock margin, the distinction between the two *cannot be overstated*, as short options positions can never be traded with borrowed money. BPR is *not* borrowed money nor does it accrue interest. It is *your* capital that is out of play for the duration of the short option trade. Margin, mostly used for stock trading, is money borrowed from brokers to purchase stock valued beyond the cash in an account. Interest *does* accrue on margin (usually between a 5% to 7% annual rate), and traders are required to pay back the margin plus interest regardless of whether the stock trade was profitable. Margin and BPR are conceptually different: Margin amplifies stock purchasing power, and BPR lowers purchasing power to account for the additional risk of short options.

The definition of BPR and its usage differs depending on whether the strategy is long or short and whether the strategy has defined or undefined risk. For long options, the maximum loss is simply the cost of the option, so that is the BPR. Defining the BPR for short options is more complicated, particularly for undefined risk positions, because the loss is theoretically unlimited. Defined risk trades, which will be covered in the next chapter, are short premium trades with a known maximum loss. These are simply short premium contracts (undefined risk trades) combined with cheaper, long premium contracts that will cap the excess losses when the underlying price moves past the further strike. BPR *is* the maximum loss for a defined risk strategy, but only an estimate for maximum loss for an undefined risk trade. Because the undefined risk case is more complicated, this chapter explains the BPR as it relates to undefined risk strategies, specifically short strangles.

Up until now, options trading has predominantly been discussed within the context of strangles, an undefined risk strategy with limited gain and theoretically unlimited loss. In this case, the BPR is calculated such that it is unlikely that the loss of a position will exceed that threshold. More specifically, BPR is intended to account for roughly 95% of potential losses with exchange-traded fund (ETF) underlyings and 90% of potential losses with stock underlyings.[1] The historical effectiveness of BPR for an ETF underlying is seen in Figure 4.1 by looking at losses for 45 days to expiration (DTE) 16Δ SPY strangle from 2005–2021.

---

[1] This statistic will vary with the IV of the underlying, but this is a suitable approximation for general cases.

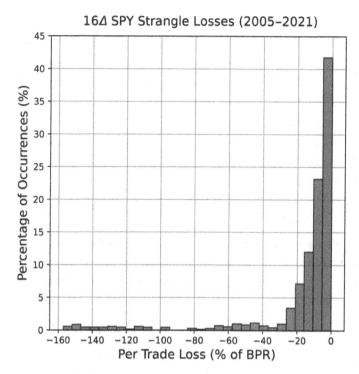

Figure 4.1 Loss as a % of BPR for 45 DTE 16Δ SPY strangles held to expiration from 2005–2021.

In this example, most losses ranged from 0% to 20% of the BPR. Roughly 95% of all these losses were accounted for by the BPR when this position was held to expiration, as expected. Though BPR did not always capture the full extent of realized losses, it is an effective proxy for worst-case loss on a trade-by-trade basis in most cases. This metric works fairly well for SPY strangles, but strangles with more volatile underlyings and strangles with tighter strikes may be more likely to have losses that breach BPR (hence the 90% efficacy rate for stocks).

BPR corresponds to the capital required to place a trade, and that quantity varies depending on the specific strategy. The BPR for short strangles can be approximated as 20% of the price of the underlying, but mathematically, BPR depends on three variables: the stock price, put/call prices, and the put/call strike prices.[2] Because the strangle is composed of the short out-of-the-money (OTM) call and short OTM put, the BPR required to sell a strangle is simply the larger of the short put BPR and the short call BPR. The short call/put BPR is the largest of three different values:

1. $((0.2 \times \text{stock price}) - |\text{strike price} - \text{stock price}|) \times 100$, which is the expected loss from a 20% move in the underlying price.
2. $0.1 \times \text{strike price} \times 100$, which is the expected loss from a 10% strike breach.
3. $250 - \text{contract price}$, which ensures that there is a minimum BPR for cheap options.

As BPR is intended to encompass the largest likely loss for an undefined risk contract, the largest of these values is taken. This can be mathematically represented using the *max* function, which takes the largest of the given values:

$$\text{Short Put BPR} = max\left(((0.2 \times S) - (S - K))\right.$$
$$\times 100, \ (0.1 \times K)$$
$$\left. \times 100, 250 - P \times 100\right) \qquad (4.1)$$

$$\text{Short Call BPR} = max\left(((0.2 \times S) - (K - S))\right.$$
$$\times 100, \ (0.1 \times K)$$
$$\left. \times 100, 250 - C \times 100\right) \qquad (4.2)$$

Combining these formulas, the BPR of the strangle is given by:

$$\text{Short Strangle BPR} = max(\text{Put BPR}, \text{Call BPR}) \qquad (4.3)$$

Clearly, this equation is hairy, but using some numerical examples, one can infer how strangle BPR and, therefore, option risk changes with more intuitive variables, such as the historical and implied volatility of the underlying. Consider three potential strangle trades outlined in Table 4.1.

---

[2] This is the FINRA (Financial Industry Regulatory Authority) regulatory minimum. Brokers typically follow this formula, but occasionally (especially when IV is very high) they will increase the capital requirements for contracts on specific underlyings.

Table 4.1   Three examples of approximate 45 DTE 16Δ strangle trades with different parameters and the resulting BPR.

	Scenario A	Scenario B	Scenario C
Stock Price	$150	$150	$300
Call Strike	$160	$175	$320
Put Strike	$140	$130	$280
Call Price	$1	$2	$2
Put Price	$1	$2	$2
BPR	$2,000	$1,750	$4,000
IV	20%	45%	20%

The underlying in Scenario B is priced the same as that of Scenario A, but the strikes for the 16Δ strangle are further apart (consistent with a higher implied volatility). The underlying in Scenario C is twice as expensive as the underlyings in Scenarios A and B, but the IV in Scenario C is the same as that of Scenario A.

Because the BPR is higher in Scenario C compared to Scenario A (but the implied volatility and contract delta are the same), traders can deduce that strangle BPR tends to increase with the price of the underlying. *Technically*, BPR is inversely correlated with option price, but the BPR still tends to increase with the price of the underlying because more expensive instruments have larger volatilities (as a dollar amount) and, therefore, higher potential losses. BPR also decreases as the IV of the underlying increases, and both relationships can be seen in Figure 4.2 looking at BPR for 45 DTE 16Δ SPY strangles from 2005–2021.

These charts show a strong linear relationship between BPR and underlying price and a slightly messier inverse relationship between BPR and underlying IV. This relationship is largely driven by the strikes moving further OTM for a fixed Δ as IV increases. BPR tends to decrease exponentially as the IV of the underlying increases, and because BPR is a rough estimate for worst-case loss, this relationship illustrates how the magnitude of potential outlier losses tends to decrease when IV increases.[3]

---

[3] This relationship between BPR and IV is specific to strangles. The next chapter discusses how these relationships may differ for certain defined risk strategies.

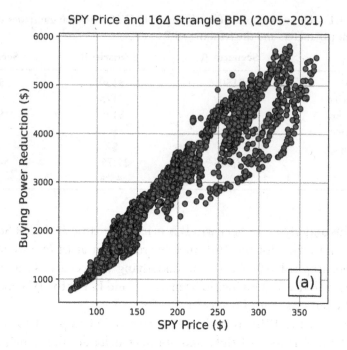

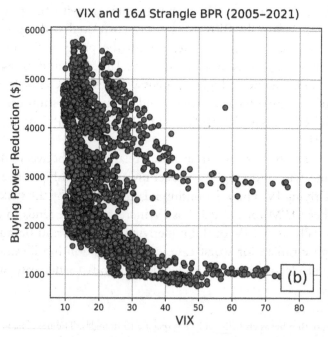

Figure 4.2 Data from 45 DTE 16Δ SPY strangles from 2005–2021. (a) BPR as a function of underlying price. (b) BPR as a function of underlying IV.

Short premium positions carry higher credits and larger profit potentials when IV is high, but the reduction in BPR also allows more short premium positions to be placed compared to when IV is low. Because average profit and loss (P/L) is higher on a trade-by-trade basis *and* more potentially profitable positions can be opened, it is essential to reserve a large percentage of portfolio buying power for high IV conditions. This additionally justifies increasing the percentage of portfolio capital allocated to short premium BPR as IV increases. These crucial high-IV profits improve portfolio performance but also cushion potential future losses. Historically, when the VIX has been over 40 compared to under 15, the same amount of capital has covered the BPR of roughly twice as many 16Δ SPY strangles. The difference between the number of short premium trades allowed in these two volatility environments is even larger when taking portfolio allocation guidelines into account. For context, consider the scenarios outlined in Table 4.2.

Table 4.2 Two portfolios with the same net liquidity but different amounts of market volatility, using SPY strangle data from 2005–2021.

	Scenario A	Scenario B
Net Portfolio Liquidity	$100,000	$100,000
Current VIX	> 40	< 15
Portfolio Allocation	$50,000	$25,000
Approx. 16Δ SPY Strangle BPR	$1,500	$3,300
Max Number of Strangles	33	7

It's important to note that BPR can be used to compare the capital at risk for variations of the same type of strategy, but it *cannot* be used to compare the risk between defined risk strategies and undefined risk strategies. For example, if the BPR required to trade a short strangle with underlying A was twice the BPR required to trade a short strangle with underlying B and otherwise had identical parameters, we can conclude that A is twice as risky as B. This is a valid comparison because we are considering two trades with the same risk profile, but BPR *cannot* be used to compare strategies with different risk profiles (say, a short strangle versus a short put) because it does not account for factors like the probability of profit or the probability of incurring a large loss. This subtlety will be discussed in more detail in the following chapter.

Understanding BPR is crucial when transitioning from options theory to applied options trading because it corresponds to the actual capital requirements of trading short options. BPR is also necessary to discuss the capital efficiency of options (option leverage) in entirety. Consider a stock trading at $100 with a volatility of 20%, and suppose a trader wanted to invest in this asset with a bullish directional assumption. The trader could achieve a bullish directional exposure to this underlying in a few different ways as shown with the examples in Table 4.3.

Table 4.3 Example trades that offer bullish directional exposure. Assume that the 50Δ (ATM) call and put contracts have 45 DTE durations and cover 100 shares of stock.

Strategy	Capital Required	Max Profit	Max Loss	Probability of Profit (POP)
50 Shares of Long Stock	$5,000	∞	$5,000	50%
Long 50Δ Call	$280	∞	$280	30%
Short 50Δ Put	$2,000 (BPR)	$280	$9,720	60%

In this one-to-one comparison, the effects of option leverage are clear because the long call position achieves the same profit potential as the long stock position with 94% less capital at risk. The short put position is capable of losing several times the initial investment of the trade but has a higher POP than the long stock position and requires 60% less capital. Suppose that the price of the stock increases to $105 after 45 days. The resulting profits and corresponding returns for these different positions is given below:

- Long stock: Profit = 50 shares × ($105 − $100) = $250
- Long ATM call: Profit = 100 shares × ($105 − $100) − $280 = $220
- Short ATM put: Profit = $280

In this example, the long call position was able to achieve 88% of the long stock profit with 94% less capital, and the short put position was able to achieve 12% *more* profit than the long stock position with 60% less capital.

Takeaways

1. Because short premiums are subject to significant tail risk, brokers must reserve capital to cover the potential losses of each position. This capital is called BPR. The total amount of portfolio capital available for trading is called portfolio buying power.

2. BPR is used to evaluate short premium risk on a trade-by-trade basis in two ways: BPR is a fairly reliable metric for worst-case loss of an undefined risk position, and BPR is used to determine if a position is appropriate for a portfolio based on its buying power.

3. For long options, BPR is the cost of the option. For short strangles, the BPR is roughly 20% of the price of the underlying. BPR for short options encompasses roughly 95% of potential losses for ETF underlyings and 90% of losses for stock underlyings.

4. Strangle BPR tends to increase linearly with the price of the underlying because more expensive instruments have larger volatilities (as a dollar amount) and, therefore, higher potential losses. There is an inverse relationship between strangle BPR and underlying IV; more specifically, it approximately decreases exponentially as the IV of the underlying increases. This demonstrates the advantages of trading short when IV is high because more short strangles can be opened with the same amount of capital as in low IV, and the outlier loss potential is generally lower.

5. BPR can be used to compare capital at risk for variations of the same strategy, but it cannot be used to compare the risk of different strategies with different risk profiles.

6. The leveraged nature of options allows traders to achieve a desired risk-return profile with significantly less capital than an equivalent stock position.

Chapter 5

Constructing a Trade

This book has covered a number of topics but how does one tie all these concepts together and actually build a trade? Options are unique in that they have *tunable* risk-reward profiles, and the type of strategy and choice of contract parameters hugely impact the characteristics of that profile. This chapter describes some common short premium strategies and how varying each contract feature tends to alter the risk-reward properties of a short position. Some basic guidelines are also included, but the ideal trade selection ultimately depends on personal profit goals, loss tolerances, account size, and the existing positions in a portfolio. Each new trade should complement existing positions, ideally contributing some degree of diversification to the overall risk profile. However, first this chapter outlines the mechanics of building individual trades; portfolio management will be discussed later.

The general procedure for constructing a trade can be summarized as follows:

1. Choose an asset universe.
2. Choose an underlying.
3. Choose a contract duration.
4. Choose a defined or undefined risk strategy.
5. Choose a directional assumption.
6. Choose a delta.

All these factors impact the overall profile of a trade, and strategies are rarely constructed in a linear manner. Traders build trades according to their personal preferences and the size of their account, making the process of constructing a position unique. For instance, if the priority is an *undefined risk* trade, the choice of underlying will have more constraints. If the priority is trading a *particular underlying under a certain directional assumption*, the delta and the risk definition will have more constraints.

Choose an Asset Universe

Before choosing an underlying, it's important to start with an appropriate asset universe or a set of tradable securities with desirable characteristics. The assets suitable for retail options trading must have highly liquid options markets, meaning the contracts for the security can be easily converted into cash without significantly affecting market price. To understand why liquidity is crucial, consider an example of an *illiquid* asset, such as a house. Selling a home at fair market value in a saturated housing market requires significant time and effort. Sellers run the additional risk of having to reduce the asking price significantly to secure a buyer quickly. Options illiquidity carries risk for similar reasons, and selectively trading assets with liquid options markets ensures that contract orders will be filled efficiently and at a fair market price.

Options liquidity is not equivalent to underlying liquidity. An underlying is considered liquid if it has the following characteristics:

- A high daily volume, meaning many shares traded daily (>1 million).
- A tight bid-ask spread, meaning a small difference between the maximum a buyer is willing to pay and the minimum a seller is willing to take (<0.1% of the asset price).

Some examples of liquid underlyings include AMZN, IBM, SPY, and TSLA, as shown in Table 5.1 below.

Table 5.1 Pricing, bid-ask spread, and daily volume data for different equities collected on February 10, 2020, at 1 p.m.

Asset	Previous Closing Price	Bid-Ask Spread	Spread/Close (% of Closing Price)	Daily Trading Volume
AMZN	$3,322.94	$0.32	0.01%	1,240,935
IBM	$121.98	$0.05	0.04%	2,484,505
SPY	$390.51	$0.02	0.005%	16,619,920
TSLA	$863.42	$0.51	0.06%	9,371,760

It is relatively straightforward to verify underlying liquidity using daily volume and bid-ask spread as a percentage of closing price. However, a liquid underlying may not have an equally liquid options market. Sufficiently liquid options underlyings must have *contract prices* with tight bid-ask spreads and high daily volumes. The options selection should also offer flexible time frames and strike prices. An underlying with a liquid options market is thus classified by the following properties:

- A high open interest or volume across strikes (at least a few hundred per strike).
- A tight bid-ask spread (<1% of the contract price).
- Available contracts with several strike prices and expiration dates.

Options liquidity ensures that traders have a wide selection of contracts to choose from and that short premium positions can be opened (i.e., contracts can be sold to a buyer) easily. Additionally, liquidity minimizes the risk of being stuck in a position because it allows traders to close short premium positions (i.e., identical contracts can be bought back) quickly.

The asset universe presented in this book is equity-based and mostly consists of stock and exchange-traded fund (ETF) underlyings, recalling that a stock represents a share of ownership for a single company, and an ETF tracks a specific set of securities, such as a sector, commodity, or market index. However, asset universes are generally product indifferent and can include any instruments with liquid options that present opportunities, such as commodities, digital currencies, and futures.

Choose an Underlying

The choice of underlying from a universe of sufficiently liquid assets is somewhat arbitrary, but traders often choose to trade short options on instruments for a preferred company, sector, or market under specific directional beliefs. Though this is a perfectly fine way to trade, it's also important to select an underlying with an appropriate amount of risk for a given account size. The two broad classes of instruments in the example asset universe, stocks and ETFs generally have different volatility profiles, and there are pros and cons to trading each, summarized in Table 5.2.

Table 5.2 General pros and cons for stock and ETF underlyings.

Stocks		ETFs	
Pros	Cons	Pros	Cons
• Tend to have options with higher credits and higher profit potentials • Frequent high implied volatility (IV) conditions	• Single-company risk factors • Earnings and dividend risk • Tend to have options with higher buying power reductions (BPRs)	• Inherently diversified across sectors or markets • Tend to have options with lower BPRs and are still highly liquid	• Limited selection compared to stocks • High IV conditions are not common

When choosing an underlying, the capital requirement of the trade is a limiting factor. A single position should generally occupy no more than 5% to 7% of portfolio capital, meaning that stock underlyings may not be suitable for small accounts because they are more expensive to trade. However, since selling premium when IV is elevated has several benefits, stock underlyings may be preferable underlyings in certain circumstances. As stocks are subject to company- and sector-specific risks, they tend to have higher IVs compared to ETFs and tend to present elevated IV opportunities more often. Note that if trading stock options, investors should also be aware of the contextual information (e.g., earnings reports dates, company announcements) that may be driving these periods of IV inflation because it may impact the strategy choice.[1] This practice is less important when trading options with ETF underlyings.

The additional risk factors (coupled with the fact that liquid stocks are often more expensive than ETFs) result in stock options generally having much larger profit and loss (P/L) swings throughout the contract duration, more ending P/L variability, and more tail risk. If the capital requirements of the trade are not excessive and the IV of the underlying is favorable, then these will be the next factors to consider. Overall, stock options are usually riskier but also carry a higher profit potential than ETF options. Consider the statistics outlined in Table 5.3.

Table 5.3   Options P/L and probability of profit (POP) statistics 45 days to expiration (DTE) 16Δ strangles with six different underlyings, held to expiration, from 2009–2020. Assets include SPY (S&P 500 ETF), GLD (gold commodity ETF), SLV (silver commodity ETF), AAPL (Apple stock), GOOGL (Google stock), and AMZN (Amazon stock).

16Δ Strangle Statistics, Held to Expiration (2009–2020)				
	Underlying	**Average Profit**	**Average Loss**	**POP**
	SPY	$160	−$297	82%
ETFs	GLD	$125	−$424	83%
	SLV	$33	−$103	81%
	AAPL	$431	−$1,425	76%
Stocks	GOOGL	$1,108	−$2,886	80%
	AMZN	$1,041	−$2,215	78%

The tolerance for P/L swings, ending P/L variability, and tail exposure depends mostly on account size and personal risk preferences. If a trade approximately satisfies those preferences and the constraints previously stated, then the choice of underlying is somewhat irrelevant because of a concept called product indifference. Because IV is derived from option price, if two assets have the same IV, their options will have roughly the same price (as a percentage of underlying price).

---

[1] IV inflation specifically due to earnings is the basis for a type of strategy called an earnings play. Earnings plays will be discussed in Chapter 9 and for now will not be part of stock options discussions.

Consequently, one underlying will not give more edge with respect to options pricing inefficiencies compared to another, provided they have similarly liquid options markets. To visualize this, consider the example in Table 5.4.

Table 5.4   Two sample options underlyings with the same IV but differing stock and put prices.

Option Parameters	Scenario A	Scenario B
Stock Price	$100	$200
IV	33%	33%
45 DTE 16Δ Put Price	$1	$2

   In Scenario A, the put is $1 (1% of the underlying price). Due to the efficient nature of options pricing, the short put in Scenario B will also cost 1% of the underlying price, as both assets have the same IV. Product indifference suggests that no one (liquid) underlying is inherently superior to another, merely that there are proportional trade-offs among different assets. The high-risk, high-reward nature of stocks is not inherently better or worse than the relatively stable nature of ETFs, but some assets may be more suitable for an individual trader than others. We can, thus, conclude that the choice of an underlying essentially depends on five main factors (in order of significance):

1. The liquidity of the options market
2. The BPR of the trade relative to account size[2]
3. The IV of the underlying[3]
4. The preferred magnitude of P/L swings, ending P/L variability, and tail exposure per trade
5. The preferred company, sector, or market exposure

---

[2] This will be explored more later in this chapter and in Chapter 7, when covering the portfolio allocation guidelines in more detail.
[3] In practice, IV is often interpreted according to the IV percentile or IV rank of the underlying. This is a more common trading metric because traders are rarely deeply familiar with the IV dynamics of different assets, and it is essential to include a range of assets in a balanced portfolio.

Choose a Contract Duration

There are many ways to choose a contract duration, but this book approaches this process from a qualitative perspective. The three primary goals when choosing a contract duration are summarized as follows:

1. Using portfolio buying power effectively.
2. Maintaining consistency and reaching a large number of occurrences.
3. Selecting a suitable time frame given contextual information.

It is essential to determine what contract duration is the most effective use of portfolio buying power without exceeding risk tolerances. Premium prices tend to be more sensitive to changes in underlying price (higher gamma) for contracts that are near expiration (5 DTE) compared to contracts that are far from expiration (120 DTE). Consequently, short-term contracts tend to have significant P/Ls swings for a larger portion of their duration compared to longer-term contracts, which initially have more moderate P/L swings and gradually become more volatile. Most contracts also tend to exhibit an increase in P/L instability as they near expiration, which is also a consequence of higher gamma. The gamma of a contract tends to increase throughout a contract's duration, usually the result of the underlying price drifting closer to one of the strangle strikes over time. Figure 5.1 illustrates these concepts by comparing the standard deviation of daily P/Ls for different durations of the same type of contract.

All of these strangles exhibit a decrease in P/L swings right before expiration. This is because options rapidly lose their extrinsic value near expiration, presuming they are not in-the-money (ITM), which is usually the case because 16Δ options often expire worthless. Near expiration, this exponential decline in premium from theta decay outweighs the magnitude of the P/L swings.

The P/L swings at the beginning of the contract vary greatly based on the contract duration. On day seven, the daily P/L for the 15 DTE contract has a high variance, and the 30 DTE, 45 DTE, and 60 DTE contracts have much lower P/L swings around the seven-day mark. This is because the 16Δ strikes in the 15 DTE contract are much closer to the

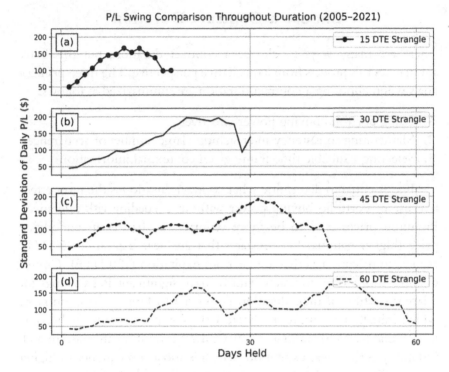

Figure 5.1 Standard deviation of daily P/Ls (in dollars) for 16Δ SPY strangles with various durations from 2005–2021. Included are durations of (a) 15 DTE, (b) 30 DTE, (c) 45 DTE and (d) 60 DTE.

at-the-money (ATM) than the 16Δ strikes in the 30+ DTE contracts. This is shown numerically in Table 5.5.[4]

Table 5.5 illustrates how the 16Δ strikes are closer to the stock price for the 15 DTE contract compared to longer duration strangles. Therefore, small changes in the price of the underlying will have a larger impact on the option's delta compared to contracts with longer durations and further out strike prices. The 30+ DTE contracts tend to experience larger P/L swings once they near expiration because the underlying price often drifts toward one of the strikes over time.

Longer contract durations, because their P/L swings are manageable for a longer period of time, give traders more time to assess the trade and adjust to changes in market conditions. However, trade durations that are

---

[4] The put distance and call distance are not symmetric. This is due to strike skew, which will be discussed later in this chapter and in the appendix.

Table 5.5   Data for 16Δ SPY strangles with different durations from April 20, 2021. The first row is the distance between the strike for a 16Δ put and the price of the underlying for different contract durations (i.e., if the price of the underlying is $100 and the strike for a 16Δ put is $95, then the put distance is ($100 − $95)/$100 = 5%). The second row is the distance between the strike for a 16Δ call and the price of the underlying for different contract durations.

16Δ SPY Option Distance from ATM

Option Type	15 DTE	30 DTE	45 DTE
Put Distance	3.9%	6.5%	8.0%
Call Distance	2.4%	3.9%	4.9%

too long are not necessarily effective uses of buying power because they do not allow for as many occurrences and take a longer time to generate profits. To summarize, longer-term contracts, which don't typically experience large changes in P/L until the latter half of their duration, tie up buying power for a long time without generating significant profit most of that time. By comparison, shorter-term contracts exhibit volatile P/L swings for the majority of their duration and leave little time to react to new conditions. A middle ground contract duration, one between 30 and 60 days on a monthly expiration cycle,[5] is considered a suitable use of buying power. Middle ground durations offer a period of manageable P/L swings while providing a fair amount of daily premium decay and a reasonable timescale for profit. This buffer time allows traders to evaluate the viability of a trade before P/L swings become more volatile. It also allows traders to incorporate different trade management strategies, which will be covered in the next chapter.

Another important factor to consider when choosing a contract duration is consistency and the number of occurrences. Consistently choosing similar contract time frames increases the number of occurrences and simplifies portfolio management because expiration and management times will roughly align for the majority of short premium trades in a portfolio. As discussed in Chapter 3, a large number of occurrences is required to reduce the variance of portfolio averages and maximize the likelihood of realizing long-term expected values.

---

[5] Common options expiration dates are divided into weekly, monthly, and quarterly cycles. Contracts with *monthly* expirations cycles are preferable because they are consistently liquid across liquid underlyings. For highly liquid assets, any expiration cycle is acceptable.

For profit and risk expectations to be dependable, it is essential to choose contract durations (and management strategies) that allow for a reasonable number of occurrences and to do so consistently. Therefore, it's good practice to choose a contract time frame that is convenient to maintain and short enough to allow for several trades to be placed throughout the trading year, presuming the duration maintains a manageable amount of tail risk exposure.

The final major factor when choosing a contract duration is contextual information, particularly when trading stock options. Contextual information, such as an approaching election, earnings report date, or forecasted natural disaster cannot necessarily be used to consistently forecast price direction, but it may indicate a predictable change in price volatility. There is, therefore, utility in taking contextual information into account when choosing a contract time frame. This will be discussed in more detail in Chapter 9.

Choose Defined or Undefined Risk

Long options strategies are defined risk trades, as the maximum loss is capped by the price of the contract. Short options positions may have defined or undefined risk profiles. Defined risk strategies have a fixed maximum loss, but capping downside risk has drawbacks. Undefined risk strategies have unlimited downside risk, meaning the maximum loss on a trade-by-trade basis is potentially unlimited. The pros and cons of defined and undefined risk strategies are outlined in Table 5.6.

Table 5.6 Comparison of defined and undefined risk strategies.

Undefined Risk		Defined Risk	
Pros	**Cons**	**Pros**	**Cons**
• Higher POPs	• Unlimited	• Limited	• Lower POPs
• Higher profit	downside risk	downside risk	• Lower profit
potentials	• Higher BPRs	• Lower BPRs	potentials
	(more expensive	(less expensive	• Can run into
	to trade)	to trade)	liquidity issues[a]

[a]Defined risk trades, because they consist of short premium and long premium contracts, require more contracts to be filled than equivalent undefined risk trades. There is, therefore, a higher risk that a defined risk order will be unable to close at a good price compared to an equivalent undefined risk position.

Defined risk strategies have a known maximum loss (i.e., the BPR of the trade) and will typically have a lower BPR than an undefined risk strategy with similar parameters (underlying, contract duration, strikes). Although defined risk positions expose less capital than equivalent undefined risk positions, this does not imply they carry less risk.

Recall from the discussion of option risk in Chapter 3 that there are several ways to quantify the risk of an options strategy. Though defined risk strategies avoid carrying *outlier risk*, they are more likely to lose most or all their BPR when losses do occur. It's, therefore, *essential* to recognize that BPR is mathematically and functionally different for defined and undefined risk trades, and it *cannot* be used as a comparative risk metric between them. This will be discussed later in the chapter.

Due to the differences in POP and profit potential between risk profiles, the maximum amount of portfolio capital allocated should differ depending on whether the strategy is defined or undefined risk. For undefined risk strategies, traders are compensated for the significant tail risk with high profit potentials and high POPs. It is generally recommended that undefined risk strategies constitute the majority of portfolio capital allocated to short premium strategies. More specifically, *at least* 75% of allocated capital should be in undefined risk strategies (with a maximum of 7% allocated per trade) and at most 25% of allocated capital should be in defined risk strategies (with a maximum of 5% allocated per trade). For a numerical example, consider the allocation scenarios for a $100,000 portfolio described in Table 5.7.

Table 5.7 Portfolio allocation for defined and undefined risk strategies with a $100,000 portfolio at different VIX levels.

VIX Level	Maximum Portfolio Allocation	Minimum Undefined Risk Allocation	Maximum Defined Risk Allocation
20	$30,000	$22,500 ($7,000 max BPR per trade)	$7,500 ($5,000 max BPR per trade)
40	$50,000	$37,500 ($7,000 max BPR per trade)	$12,500 ($5,000 max BPR per trade)

These differences will be elaborated on in the next section, but to summarize, the following five factors are generally the most important to consider when comparing defined and undefined risk trades:

1. The amount of BPR required for a trade relative to the net liquidity of the portfolio.
2. The likelihood of profiting from a position.
3. The preferred amount of downside risk.
4. The preferred ending P/L variability and preferred magnitude of P/L swings throughout the contract duration.
5. The profit targets.

Defined risk trades typically require less capital, have more moderate P/L swings throughout the trade, and have less ending P/L standard deviation compared to undefined risk trades. Consequently, defined risk trades may be preferable for small accounts and relatively new traders. Undefined risk trades are statistically favorable and have, therefore, been the focus of this book. However, the following section discusses how to construct defined risk trades that behave like undefined risk trades while offering protection against extreme losses. For these types of strategies, and only these types of strategies, defined risk trades can be substituted for undefined risk trades in the portfolio allocation guidelines.

Choose a Directional Assumption

After choosing a contract underlying, duration, and risk profile, the next steps are determining the directional assumption for the price of the underlying asset and selecting a strategy consistent with that belief and the preferred risk profile. The directional assumption may be bullish, bearish or neutral, and the optimal choice is subjective and depends on one's interpretation of the efficient market hypothesis (EMH). Recall that the EMH assumes that current prices reflect some degree of available information and comes in three main forms:

1. Weak EMH: Current prices reflect all past price information.
2. Semi-strong EMH: Current prices reflect all publicly available information.
3. Strong EMH: Current prices reflect all possible information.

Each form of the EMH implies some degree of limitation with respect to price predictability:

- Weak EMH: Past price information cannot be used to consistently predict future price information, which invalidates technical analysis.
- Semi-strong EMH: Any publicly available information cannot be used to consistently predict future price information, which invalidates fundamental analysis.
- Strong EMH: No information can be used to consistently predict future price information, which invalidates insider trading.

No form of the EMH is universally accepted or rejected, and the ideal form to trade under (if any) depends on personal preference. This book takes a semi-strong approach to market predictability, assuming equity and option prices effectively reflect available information and that few directional assumptions are valid (e.g., the market trends bullish in the long term). As volatility reverts back to a long-term value following significant deviations, it is more valid to make directional assumptions on IV once it's inflated rather than directional assumptions around equity prices. This book, therefore, typically focuses on directionally *neutral* strategies, such as the short strangle, because these types of positions profit from changes in volatility and time and are relatively insensitive to price changes. However, that is a personal choice. Multiple strategies are outlined in Table 5.8.

For reasons discussed in earlier chapters, all these strategies perform best in high IV. However, the POPs of these trades remain relatively high in all volatility environments, justifying that some percentage of capital should be allocated in all IV conditions.

To elaborate on the differences between defined and undefined risk, compare statistics for the two neutral strategies: the iron condor and the strangle. An iron condor consists of a short out-of-the-money (OTM) vertical call spread and a short OTM vertical put spread (introduced in Table 5.8). This trade is effectively a short strangle paired with a long strangle having strikes that are further OTM (typically called wings). As with strangles, iron condors are profitable when the underlying price stays within the range defined by the short strikes or when there is a significant IV contraction or time decay. For example, a 16Δ strangle can be turned

Table 5.8 Examples of popular short options strategies with the same delta of approximately 20.[a]

Strategy	Composition	Defined or Undefined Risk	Directional Assumption	POP[b]
Naked Option	Short OTM put	Undefined	Bullish	80%
	Short OTM call	Undefined	Bearish	80%
Vertical Spread	Short OTM put, long further OTM put	Defined	Bullish	77%
	Short OTM call, long further OTM put	Defined	Bearish	77%
Strangle	Short OTM put, short OTM call	Undefined	Neutral	70%
Iron Condor	Short OTM vertical call spread, short OTM vertical put spread	Defined	Neutral	60%

[a]The directional assumption will be flipped for the long side of a non-neutral position. For a long neutral position, the assumption is that the underlying price will move outside of the price range defined by the contract strikes. The POP of the long side is given by 1 − (short POP).

[b]These POPs are approximate. The POP of a defined risk strategy depends heavily on the choice of long delta(s). Contracts with wider long deltas will generally have higher POPs. This will be explored more later in the chapter.

into a 16Δ *iron condor with 10Δ wings*[6] with the addition of a long call and a long put with the same duration, further from OTM (the long contracts are 10Δ in this case). An example of an iron condor is shown in Table 5.9 and Figure 5.2.

The long wings of the iron condor cap the maximum loss as either the difference between the strike prices of the vertical put spread or vertical call spread (whichever is greater) times the number of shares in the contract (typically 100) minus the net credit. The maximum loss of the short iron condor is equivalently the BPR required to open the trade.

---

[6] Recall that smaller deltas are further from ATM than larger deltas.

Table 5.9 Example of a 16Δ SPY strangle and a 16Δ SPY iron condor with 10Δ wings when the price of SPY is $315 and its IV is 12%. All contracts must have the same duration.

Contract Strikes	16Δ Strangle	16Δ Iron Condor with 10Δ Wings
Long Call Strike	---	$332
Short Call Strike	$328	$328
Short Put Strike	$302	$302
Long Put Strike	---	$298

The short strikes were approximated with the expected range formula and the long strikes for the iron condor wings were approximated with the Black-Scholes formula. Underlyings are often subject to strike skew, not to be confused with distribution skew, which neither of these methods really consider. This means that the strikes (both long and short) are typically not equidistant (as a dollar amount) from the price of the underlying although they were approximated in this example as such. This concept will be explored more later in the chapter.

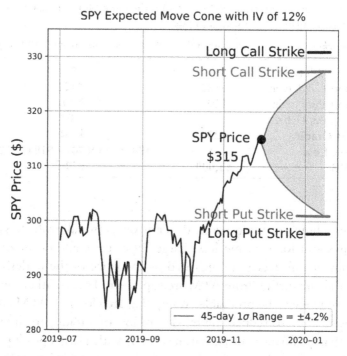

Figure 5.2 Graphical representation of the iron condor described in Table 5.9. The 10Δ wings correspond to long strikes that are $17 from ATM, which is further OTM than the 16Δ short strikes that are $13 from ATM.

It can be summarized by the following formula:

$$\begin{aligned}
\text{Short Iron Condor BPR} \\
= 100 \times \textit{max}(\text{long call strike} - \text{short call strike}, \\
\text{short put strike} - \text{long put strike}) \\
- 100 \times (\text{short call price} + \text{short put price} \\
- \text{long call price} - \text{long put price})
\end{aligned} \quad (5.1)$$

Continuing with the same example as shown in Table 5.9, we apply this formula to calculate some statistics for these two trades in Table 5.10.

Table 5.10 Initial credits for the 16Δ SPY strangle and the 16Δ SPY iron condor with 10Δ wings outlined in Table 5.9. Because the difference between the vertical call spread strikes ($332–$328) and the vertical put spread strikes ($302–$298) is the same ($4), this value is used when calculating the maximum loss.

Contract Credits	16Δ Strangle	16Δ Iron Condor with 10Δ Wings
Long Call Debit	---	−$69
Short Call Credit	$122	$122
Short Put Credit	$108	$108
Long Put Debit	---	−$57
Net Credit	$230	$104
Max Loss	∞	(100 *shares* × $4) − $104 = $296
BPR	$5,000	$296

The choice of wing width depends on personal profit targets and the threshold for extreme loss. Large losses generally occur once the long put or call strikes are breached by the price of the underlying, so wings that are further from ATM are exposed to larger outlier moves but are more likely to be profitable. Wings that are closer to ATM are more expensive but also reduce the maximum loss of a trade. To summarize, wings that are further out yield iron condors with a larger profit potential and a higher probability of profit but also larger possible losses. For some numerical examples, refer to the statistics in Table 5.11.

Table 5.11 Statistical comparison of 45 DTE 16Δ SPY iron condors with different wing widths, held to expiration from 2005–2021. Wings that have a smaller delta are further from ATM compared to wings with a larger delta. Included are 45 DTE 16Δ SPY strangle statistics held to expiration from 2005–2021 for comparison.

16Δ Iron Condor Statistics (2005–2021)				16Δ Strangle Statistics (2005–2021)
Statistics	5Δ Wings	10Δ Wings	13Δ Wings	
POP	79%	75%	73%	81%
Average P/L	$35	$15	$6	$44
Standard Deviation of P/L	$251	$132	$74	$614
Conditional Value at Risk (CVaR) (5%)	−$771	−$399	−$220	−$1,535

If the account size allows for it, it is preferable to trade iron condors with *wide wings*, which have more tail risk than narrow iron condors but are historically more profitable. While iron condors with narrow wings have POPs near 70%, wide iron condors may have POPs of nearly 80%, as shown in Table 5.11. Wider iron condors, although they have higher BPR requirements, are also less likely to reach max loss than tighter iron condors when losses do occur.

Defined risk strategies tend to have lower POPs and profit potentials compared to undefined risk strategies as shown by the strangle statistics included for reference. The iron condor has roughly a third of the profit potential as the strangle on average (in the case of 10Δ wings), but it also has roughly a third of the P/L standard deviation and significantly less tail exposure. Also, as in the wide iron condor example, defined risk trades can be constructed to have similar POPs as an undefined risk strategy while still offering protection from outlier losses. Defining risk in low IV, particularly with strategies that have high POPs, is one way to manage the outlier loss exposure while capitalizing on the benefits of short premium. Defined risk strategies also come with the added benefit of being significantly cheaper to trade, which is another reason they may be a more effective use of portfolio buying power when IV is low. For a numeric reference, consider the BPR statistics in Table 5.12.

Table 5.12 Average BPR comparison of 45 DTE 16Δ SPY strangles and 45 DTE 16Δ SPY iron condors with 10Δ wings when held to expiration using data from 2005–2021.

SPY Strangle and Iron Condor BPRs (2005–2021)

VIX Range	Strangle BPR	Iron Condor BPR[a]
0–15	$3,270	$363
15–25	$2,641	$426
25–35	$2,261	$585
35–45	$1,648	$553
45+	$1,445	$615

[a]Iron condors with static dollar wings (e.g., $10 wings, $20 wings) have BPRs that decrease with IV as seen with strangles. Iron condors with dynamic wings that change with variables, such as IV (e.g., 10Δ, 5Δ) have BPRs that increase with IV. Recall that the iron condor BPR is the widest short spread width minus the initial credit. Therefore, as IV increases, the widest width increases faster than the initial credit, so the BPR increases with IV.

Defined risk strategies *with high POPs* can account for a greater percentage of portfolio allocation than defined risk strategies with lower POPs. Previously, we stated that at least 75% of allocated capital should be in undefined risk strategies (with a maximum of 7% allocated per trade) and at most 25% of allocated capital should be in defined risk strategies (with a maximum of 5% allocated per trade). However, a defined risk strategy with a POP comparable to an undefined risk strategy can share undefined risk portfolio buying power, which protects capital from extreme losses while still allowing for consistent profits. Once IV expands, traders can then transition to strangles to capitalize on the higher credits and reduced outlier risk.

It's crucial to reiterate that BPR *cannot* be used to compare risk between strategies with different risk profiles. For instance, refer back to the example in Table 5.10. The strangle requires roughly 17 times more buying power than the iron condor, but this is not to say that the risk of the strangle is equivalent to the risk of 17 iron condors. The strangle is more likely to be profitable and much less likely to lose the entire BPR because that would require a much larger move in the underlying (20%) compared to the iron condor (5%). Very wide iron condors have similar risk profile to strangles, but it is generally good practice to avoid directly comparing defined and undefined risk strategies using buying power.

Choosing a Delta

Recall that delta is a measure of *directional exposure*. According to the mathematical definition derived from the Black-Scholes model, it represents the expected change in the option price given a $1 increase in the price of the underlying (assuming all other variables stay constant).[7] For example, if the price of an underlying increases by $1, the price for a long call option with a delta of 0.50 (denoted as 50Δ) will increase by approximately $0.50 per share, and the price for a long put option with a delta of −0.50 (denoted as −50Δ, or just 50Δ when the sign is clear from context) will decrease by approximately $0.50 per share.[8] The delta of a contract additionally represents the *perceived* risk of that option in terms of shares of equity. More specifically, delta corresponds to the number of shares required to hedge the directional exposure of that option according to market sentiment.

This book frequently references the 16Δ SPY strangle, which is a delta neutral trade consisting of a short 16Δ put directionally hedged with a short 16Δ call. Delta neutral positions profit from factors such as decreases in IV and time decay rather than directional changes in the underlying. When originally presented in Chapter 3, the short strike prices were related to the expected range, and therefore, strike prices were shown to be equidistant from the price of the underlying as in Figure 5.3.

The strikes in this example were derived from the expected move range approximation shown in Chapter 2. However, in practice the strikes for a 16Δ SPY put/call are calculated from real-time supply and demand and are often subject to *strike skew*. Revisit the example from Table 5.5 to see an example of this.

Table 5.5 shows that the put strikes are much further from the price of the underlying compared to the call strikes even though the call and put contracts are both 16Δ. According to market demand, put contracts further OTM have equivalent risk as call contracts less OTM. This skew

---

[7] For contracts with deltas between approximately 10 and 40, delta can also be used as a *very* rough proxy for the probability that an option will expire ITM. For instance, a 25Δ put has about a 25% chance of expiring ITM, meaning that there is a 75% POP for the short put. A 16Δ strangle is composed of a 16Δ put and a 16Δ call, so there is approximately a 32% chance that it will expire ITM (consistent with the 68% POP for the short strangle).

[8] Delta is between 0 and 1 for long calls and between −1 and 0 for long puts. For short calls and short puts, the numbers are flipped.

Figure 5.3   The price of SPY in the last 5 months of 2019. Included is the 45-day expected move cone calculated from the IV of SPY in December 2019, where the strike for the 16Δ call is $328 and the strike for the 16Δ put is $302.

results from market fear to the *downside*, meaning the market fears larger extreme moves to the downside more than extreme moves to the upside.[9] As delta is based on the market's perception of risk, strikes for a given delta are skewed according to that perception. But not all instruments will have the same degree of skew. Stocks like AAPL and GOOGL have fairly equidistant strikes, but market indexes and commodities (e.g., gold and oil) tend to have downside skew, otherwise known as put skew. Assets like GME (GameStop) and AMC (entertainment company) developed upside skew, otherwise known as call skew, during 2020.

Because delta is a measure of perceived risk in terms of share equivalency, the chosen delta is going to significantly impact the risk-reward

---

[9] This is mainly the result of the history of extreme market crashes, such as the 1987 Black Monday crash, the 2008 housing crisis, and the 2020 sell-off. Prior to 1987, the put and call strikes of the same delta were much closer to equidistant.

profile of a trade. Positions with larger deltas (closer to −100Δ or +100Δ) are more sensitive to changes in the price of the underlying compared to positions with smaller deltas (closer to 0). To observe how this impacts per-trade performance, consider the statistics for 45 DTE SPY strangles with different deltas outlined in Tables 5.13–5.15.

Table 5.13 Statistical comparison of 45 DTE SPY strangles of different deltas, held to expiration from 2005–2021.

SPY Strangle Statistics (2005–2021)

Statistics	16Δ	20Δ	30Δ
POP	81%	76%	68%
Average P/L	$44	$49	$54
Standard Deviation of P/L	$614	$659	$747
CVaR (5%)	−$1,535	−$1,673	−1,931

Table 5.14 Average BPRs of 45 DTE SPY strangles with different deltas, sorted by IV from 2005–2021.

SPY Strangle BPRs (2005–2021)

VIX Range	16Δ	20Δ	30Δ
0–15	$3,270	$3,366	$3,573
15–25	$2,641	$2,756	$3,014
25–35	$2,261	$2,415	$2,794
35–45	$1,648	$1,715	$2,058
45+	$1,445	$1,421	$1,520

Table 5.15 Probability of incurring a loss exceeding the BPR for 45 DTE SPY strangles of different deltas, held to expiration from 2005–2021.

SPY Strangle Statistics (2005–2021)

Strangle Delta	Probability of Loss Greater Than BPR
16Δ	0.90%
20Δ	0.93%
30Δ	1.0%

Positions with higher deltas have larger P/L swings throughout the contract duration, more ending P/L variability, higher BPRs and lower POPs compared to positions with lower deltas. However, higher delta positions also carry higher credits and larger profit potentials overall. Positions with lower deltas achieve smaller profits more often and are lower risk than higher delta trades. Positions with lower deltas also tend to have higher thetas as a percentage of the option value, meaning they may reach profit targets more quickly than positions with higher deltas (not shown in these tables).

The optimal choice of delta depends on the personal profit goals and, most importantly, personal risk tolerances. ITM options (options with a delta magnitude larger than 50) generally carry more directional risk and an insufficient amount of theta (expected daily profits due to time decay) than what is suitable for a short premium trade. OTM options are typically better candidates. When trading short premium, contract deltas between 10Δ and 40Δ are typically large enough to achieve reasonable growth but small enough to have manageable P/L swings, moderate standard deviation of ending P/L, and moderate outlier risk. More risk-tolerant traders generally trade options over 25Δ and more risk-averse traders will trade under 25Δ. When IV increases and options become cheaper to trade, more risk-tolerant traders may also scale delta *up* to capitalize on the larger credits across the entire options chain. It is also good practice to re-center the deltas of existing positions when IV increases because increases in IV cause the strike price for a given delta to move *further away* from the spot price. To see an example of this, consider Table 5.16.

Table 5.16   Comparison of strike prices for two 30 DTE 16Δ call options with the same underlying price but different IVs.

Example Parameters for a 30 DTE 16Δ Call Option		
IV	Underlying Price	Strike Price
10%	$100	$103
50%	$100	$117

The strike price for a 16Δ call is $17 away from the price of the underlying when the IV is 50%, compared to $3 away when the IV is 10%.

This is because an increase in IV indicates an increase in the expected range for the underlying price. When this expected range becomes larger, contracts with strikes further away from the current price of the underlying are in higher demand than in lower IV conditions. This demand increases the premiums of those contracts and consequently the perceived risk. When IV increases, it is good practice to close existing positions and reopen them with adjusted strikes that better reflect the new volatility conditions.

Takeaways

1. Constructing a trade has six major steps, and the ideal choices are based on account size and the personal profit goals, risk tolerances, and market assumptions. The primary factors to consider are the asset universe, the underlying, the contract duration, the risk profile of the strategy, the directional assumption, and the delta.

2. Traders should choose assets with highly liquid options markets, consisting of contracts that can be easily converted into cash without a significant impact on market price. Liquid options markets have a high volume across strikes, tight bid-ask spreads, and available contracts with several strike prices and expiration dates.

3. In an equity-focused asset universe, traders have two main choices of equity underlyings: stocks and ETFs. Options with stock underlyings tend to have higher credits, higher profit potentials, and more frequent high IV conditions, but they also have single-company risks and cost more to trade than options with ETF underlyings. ETFs are inherently diversified and are cheaper than stocks while being very liquid, but fewer choices are available and high IV conditions are less common.

4. A suitable contract duration should use buying power effectively, allow for consistency and a reasonable number of occurrences, and reflect the timescale of contextual events, such as upcoming earnings reports and forecasted natural disasters. Contract durations ranging from 30 to 60 days are generally a suitable use of portfolio buying power, offering manageable P/L volatility and a reasonable timescale for profit.

5. Short premium strategies may have defined or undefined risk. Undefined risk trades have higher POPs and higher profit potentials but also unlimited downside risk and higher BPRs, making them more expensive to trade. Defined risk strategies have limited downside risk and lower BPRs but also lower POPs and lower profit potentials with possible liquidity issues. High-POP defined risk strategies, such as wide iron condors, can occupy the capital reserved for undefined risk trades, and this is a particularly good strategy when IV is low. Trading high-POP defined risk trades in low IV and transitioning to undefined risk in high IV is an effective way to protect capital from outlier moves while profiting consistently.

6. Traders must choose one of three directional assumptions for the underlying price: bullish, bearish, and neutral. The optimal choice is subjective and depends on individual interpretation of the EMH, which assumes current prices reflect some degree of available information.

7. The delta of a contract represents the perceived risk of the option in terms of shares of equity, making the choice of delta based on personal risk tolerances and profit goals. A higher delta OTM contract is closer to ATM and more sensitive to changes in underlying price, meaning that these positions are generally riskier but have higher profit potentials. Lower delta OTM contracts are further from ATM and have more moderate P/L swings throughout the contract with lower ending P/L standard deviation generally. When trading short premium, ITM contracts are generally not suitable due to their high directional risks and low thetas. Contracts between 10Δ and 40Δ are generally large enough to achieve a reasonable amount of growth but small enough to have manageable P/L swings and moderate ending P/L variability.

Chapter 6

Managing Trades

Options traders can hold a position to expiration or close it prior to expiration (active management). Compared to holding a contract until expiration, an active management strategy should be considered for the following reasons:

- It allows for more occurrences over a given time frame (if capital is redeployed).
- It may allow for a more efficient use of portfolio buying power (if capital is redeployed).
- It tends to reduce risk on a trade-by-trade basis.

Trades can be managed in any number of ways, but similar to choosing a contract duration, *consistency* is essential for reaching a large number of occurrences and realizing favorable long-term averages. This book advocates for adopting a simple management strategy that is easily maintainable:

- Closing a trade at a fixed point in the contract duration.

- Closing a trade at a fixed profit or loss target.
- Some combination of these strategies.

This chapter discusses different management strategies, compares trade-by-trade performance, and elaborates on the major factors to consider when choosing appropriate position management. Because management strategies impact the proportion of initial credit traders ultimately collect, the statistics will often be represented as an initial credit percentage rather than dollars. This chapter also predominantly focuses on undefined risk strategy management. Many of these principles also apply to defined risk positions, but defined risk positions are generally more forgiving from the perspective of trade management because they occupy a smaller percentage of portfolio buying power and have limited loss potential.

Managing According to DTE

As mentioned in Chapters 3 and 5, trade profit and loss (P/L) swings tend to become more volatile as options approach expiration. For a strangle, this increase generally results from the price of the underlying drifting toward one of the strikes throughout the contract duration. Consequently, closing a trade prior to expiration, whether at a fixed point in the contract duration or at a specific profit or loss target, tends to reduce ending P/L standard deviation and outlier risk exposure on a trade-by-trade basis. Managing trades actively also frees portfolio buying power from existing positions, which can then be allocated more strategically as opportunities arise. The freed capital can be redeployed to the same type of initial position (increasing the number of occurrences)[1] *or* to a new position with more favorable short premium conditions (which may be a more efficient use of buying power).

Managing a trade according to days to expiration (DTE), such as closing a position halfway to expiration, offers the benefits described previously and is straightforward to execute. This technique has a clear management timeline and requires minimal portfolio supervision, particularly when portfolio positions have comparable durations.

---

[1] This technique is commonly known as rolling.

The choice of management time greatly affects the profit potential and outlier risk exposure of a trade because trades managed closer to expiration are more likely to be profitable and have larger profits on average but are generally exposed to more tail risk. The trade-by-trade statistics shown in Table 6.1 compare the performance of different management times for 45 DTE 16Δ SPY strangles.

Table 6.1 Statistics for 45 DTE 16Δ SPY strangles from 2005–2021 managed at different times in the contract duration.

16Δ SPY Strangle Statistics (2005–2021)

Management DTE	Probability of Profit (POP)	Average P/L	Average Daily P/L	P/L Standard Deviation	Conditional Value at Risk (CVaR) (5%)
40 DTE	67%	2.3%	$0.23	73%	−206%
30 DTE	73%	10%	$1.75	88%	−212%
21 DTE	79%	21%	$1.60	96%	−283%
15 DTE	78%	25%	$1.51	105%	−304%
5 DTE[a]	82%	33%	$1.34	185%	−514%
Expiration	81%	28%	$1.29	247%	−708%

[a]Strangles managed at 5 DTE seem to outperform strangles held to expiration because they have a higher POP and average P/L but lower P/L volatility and less tail risk. These results are specific to this strategy and data set, and were likely skewed by significant historical events. This trend is not generalizable across strategies, including the one presented in this table.

Table 6.1 shows that managing a trade prior to expiration is less likely to profit but also has less P/L standard deviation and less tail risk, and it also collects more daily, on average, compared to holding to expiration. These statistics also demonstrate that management time generally carries a trade-off among profit potential, loss potential, and the number of occurrences. Compared to trades managed earlier in the contract duration, trades managed later have larger profits and losses and also allow for fewer occurrences. As early-managed positions accommodate more occurrences and average more P/L per day than positions held to expiration, closing positions prior to expiration and redeploying capital to new positions is generally a more efficient use of capital compared to extracting more extrinsic value from an existing position.

If adopting this strategy, choose a management time that satisfies individual trade-by-trade risk tolerances, offers a suitable profit potential, and occupies buying power for a reasonable amount of time. Remember that selling premium in any capacity carries tail risk exposure even when a position is closed almost immediately (see the 40 DTE results in Table 6.1). To achieve a decent amount of long-term profit and justify the tail loss exposure, consider closing trades around the contract duration midpoint.

Managing According to a Profit or Loss Target

Compared to allowing a trade to expire, managing a position according to a profit target simplifies profit expectations and tends to reduce per-trade P/L variance. Closing limit orders can be set by a trader and automatically executed by the broker, but this management strategy still requires some active maintenance. This is because trades may never reach the predetermined profit benchmark and may require alternative management prior to expiration. Additionally, there is some subtlety in choosing the profit target because that choice significantly impacts the profit and loss potential of a trade, as shown in Tables 6.2 and 6.3.

Table 6.2   Statistics for 45 DTE 16Δ SPY strangles from 2005–2021 managed at different profit targets. If the profit target is not reached during the contract duration, the strangle expires. The final row includes statistics for 45 DTE 16Δ SPY strangles managed around halfway to expiration (21 DTE) as a reference.

16Δ SPY Strangle Statistics (2005–2021)

Profit Target	POP	Average P/L	P/L Standard Deviation	Probability of Reaching Target	CVaR (5%)
25% or Exp.	96%	11%	191%	96%	−522%
50% or Exp.	91%	16%	236%	90%	−654%
75% or Exp.	84%	22%	245%	80%	−699%
100% (Exp.)	81%	28%	247%	52%	−708%
21 DTE	79%	21%	96%	N/A	−283%

These tests did not account for whether a P/L target was reached throughout the trading day, but rather whether a target was reached by the end of the trading day. Therefore, these statistics are not entirely representative of this management technique.

Managing at a profit threshold or expiration generally carries more P/L standard deviation and outlier risk exposure on a trade-by-trade basis than managing at 21 DTE, although it also comes with higher POPs

Table 6.3 Average daily P/L and average duration for the contracts and management strategies described in Table 6.2.

16Δ SPY Strangle Statistics (2005–2021)

Profit Target	Average Daily P/L Over Average Duration	Average Duration (Days)
25% or Exp.	$1.75	15
50% or Exp.	$1.67	24
75% or Exp.	$1.49	34
100% (Exp.)	$1.29	44
21 DTE	$1.60	24

These tests did not account for whether a P/L target was reached throughout the trading day, but rather whether a target was reached by the end of the trading day. Therefore, these statistics are not entirely representative of this management technique. Additionally, because there can be significant variability in when a contract reaches a certain profit threshold, daily P/L estimates were derived from data over the average duration of the trade.

and higher per-trade profit potentials depending on the profit benchmark. Short options are highly likely to reach low profit targets early in the contract duration when P/L swings and tail risk are both fairly low. Therefore, managing a trade according to a low profit target yields a higher strategy POP, lower P/L standard deviation, and less outlier risk compared to managing at a high profit target. However, despite the higher average daily P/Ls, setting the profit threshold *too low* does not allow traders to collect a sufficient credit to justify the inherent tail risk of the position. Average P/Ls are well below the given profit target in all cases due to the tail loss potential. When using a 25% target, for example, the contract failed to reach the target only 4% of the time. Still, those losses were significant enough to bring down the P/L average by more than half. If this management strategy is adopted, a profit threshold between 50% and 75% of the initial credit is suitable to realize a reasonable amount of long-term average profit and reduce the impact of outlier losses. Additionally, because these mid-range profit targets tend to be reached near the contract midpoint or shortly after, these benchmarks also allow for a reasonable number of occurrences.[2]

---

[2] For defined risk positions, a profit target of roughly 50% or lower is more suitable because P/L swings are less volatile and higher profit targets are less likely to be reached.

Just as trades can be managed according to a fixed profit target, they can also be managed according to a fixed loss limit (a stop loss). Defining a loss limit is trickier because option P/L swings are highly volatile. Small loss limits are reached commonly, but trades are also likely to recover. Implementing a very small loss limit may significantly limit upside growth and make losses more likely. To understand this, see Table 6.4.

Table 6.4 Statistics for 45 DTE 16Δ SPY strangles from 2005–2021 managed at different loss limits. If the loss limit is not reached during the contract duration, the strangle expires. The final two rows reference other management strategies for comparison.

16Δ SPY Strangle Statistics (2005–2021)

Loss Limits	POP	Avg P/L	P/L Standard Deviation	Prob. of Reaching Target	CVaR (5%)
−50% or Exp.	58%	21%	90%	40%	−168%
−100% or Exp.	69%	25%	110%	25%	−238%
−200% or Exp.	76%	27%	131%	13%	−338%
−300% or Exp.	79%	27%	149%	8%	−450%
−400% or Exp.	79%	27%	160%	6%	−536%
None (Exp.)	81%	28%	247%	N/A	−708%
21 DTE	79%	21%	96%	N/A	−283%
50% Profit or Exp.	91%	16%	236%	90%	−654%

These tests did not account for whether or not a P/L amount was reached throughout the trading day, but rather whether it was reached by the end of the trading day. Therefore, these statistics are not entirely representative of this management technique.

Using a low stop loss threshold, −50% for example, results in lower P/L standard deviation and outlier risk compared to holding the contract to expiration. However, in this case, losses are more common and occur roughly 42% of the time since it is not uncommon for options to reach this loss threshold, although many positions ultimately recover prior to expiration (note the higher POPs for larger limits). Implementing a stop loss also does not necessarily eliminate *all* tail risk exceeding that threshold. For example, despite having a stop loss of −50%, a sudden implied volatility (IV) expansion or underlying price change may cause daily loss to increase from −25% to −75%, resulting in the closure of the trade but with a final P/L past the loss threshold. Because upside potential is limited and some degree of tail exposure exists with a very small stop loss, a mid-range stop loss of at least −200% is practical.[3] Using a stop loss and otherwise holding to expiration generally has a higher profit and larger loss potential than managing at the duration midpoint but tends to carry less tail risk than managing at a reasonable profit target. For more active trading, stop losses are not typically used alone but rather combined with another management strategy.

Comparing Management Techniques and Choosing a Strategy

The strangle management strategies presented thus far are relatively straightforward. These techniques can be ranked according to loss potential (from highest to lowest) and quantified using CVaR and P/L standard deviation of the positions studied:

1. Hold until expiration.
2. Manage at a profit target between 50% and 75%.
3. Manage at a loss limit of −200%.
4. Manage at 21 DTE (halfway to expiration).

Remember that consistency and ease of implementation are important factors to consider when choosing a management strategy. For traders who are comfortable with active trading, strategies can be combined and more precisely tuned according to individual preferences. For instance, suppose a trader of 45 DTE 16Δ SPY strangles wants a management strategy with a high POP, moderate P/L standard deviation, and moderate outlier exposure. One possibility is managing at 50% of the initial credit *or* at 21 DTE, whichever occurs first. The statistics for this strategy are outlined in Table 6.5.

---

[3] Stop losses are not suitable for defined risk strategies. As defined risk strategies have a fixed maximum loss, it is best to allow defined risk losers to expire rather than manage them at a specific loss threshold. This gives the position more opportunity to recover.

Table 6.5 Statistics for 45 DTE 16Δ SPY strangles from 2005–2021 managed either at 50% of the initial credit *or* 21 DTE, whichever comes first. Statistics for other strategies are given for comparison and ranked by CVaR.

		16Δ SPY Strangle Statistics (2005–2021)			
Management Strategy	POP	Average P/L	Average Daily P/L	P/L Standard Deviation	CVaR (5%)
21 DTE	79%	21%	$1.60	96%	−283%
21 DTE or 50% Profit	81%	18%	$1.67	96%	−288%
−200% Loss or Exp.	76%	27%	N/A	131%	−338%
50% Profit or Exp.	91%	16%	$1.67	236%	−654%
None (Exp.)	81%	28%	$1.29	247%	−708%

In this example, the duration and profit targets are moderate, resulting in a combined strategy with smaller but slightly more likely profits than 21 DTE management and significantly less loss potential than 50% profit management. This may be appealing to risk-averse traders because it eliminates a large fraction of the historic losses and significantly reduces tail exposure with the benefit of a slightly higher POP and higher average daily P/L.

When choosing a management strategy, know that all management strategies come with trade-offs among POP, average P/L, P/L standard deviation, and loss potential. How these factors are weighted depends on individual goals:

- For *likely* profits, profit potential must be smaller or exposure to outlier losses must be larger.
- For *large* profits, there must be fewer occurrences or more exposure to outlier losses.
- For a *small* loss potential, profit potential must be smaller or profits must be less likely.

For a qualitative comparison of the different strategies, see Table 6.6.

As mentioned, a suitable management strategy depends on individual preferences for trading engagement, per-trade P/L potential, P/L

Table 6.6 Qualitative comparison of different management strategies.

	Management Strategy			
	21 DTE	50% or Exp.	−200% or Exp.	Exp.
Convenience	Med	High[a]	High	High
POP	Med	High	Med	Med
Per-Trade Loss Potential	Low	High	Low	High
Per-Trade Profit Potential	Med	Low	High	High
Number of Occurrences	Med	Med	Low	Low

[a]If limit orders are used, profit target management is very convenient.

likelihood and number of occurrences. Following are example scenarios highlighting different management profiles:

- For passive traders with portfolios that can accommodate more outlier risk, it may make more sense to use only a stop loss and otherwise hold trades to expiration to extract as much extrinsic value from existing positions as possible.
- Active traders with portfolios that can accommodate more outlier risk may manage general positions at a fixed profit target and close higher-risk, higher-reward trades halfway to expiration.
- Very active traders may manage all undefined risk contracts at either 50% of the initial credit *or* halfway through the contract duration because this method prioritizes moderating outlier risk and achieving likely profits of reasonable size.

Generally speaking, an active management approach is more suitable for retail traders because more occurrences can be achieved in a given time frame, it is a more efficient use of capital, average daily profits are higher, and the per-trade loss potential is lower. It's critical to reiterate that this risk is on a *trade-by-trade* basis. Short premium losses happen infrequently and are often caused by unexpected events, making it difficult to precisely compare long-term performance of strategies of varying timescales. The next section discusses in more detail why comparing the long-term risks for management strategies is not straightforward.

A Note about Long-Term Risk

As mentioned previously, contracts tend to have more volatile P/L swings as the contract approaches expiration. Managing trades prior to expiration, therefore, tends to have lower P/L standard deviation and outlier risk exposure on a trade-by-trade basis compared to holding the contract to expiration. But it's critical to note that this reduction in risk on a trade-by-trade basis *does not necessarily translate to a reduction in risk on a long-term basis.* Though early management techniques reduce loss magnitude *per trade*, inherent risk factors arise from a larger number of occurrences. Consequently, one management strategy may have lower per-trade exposure compared to another, but it may have more *cumulative* long-term risk. Consider the scenarios outlined in Figures 6.1 and 6.2. Each scenario compares the performances of two portfolios, each with $100,000 of capital invested. Both portfolios consist of short 45 DTE 16Δ SPY strangles continuously traded, but the trades in one portfolio are managed halfway to expiration (21 DTE) and the trades in the other are managed at expiration. The unique market conditions in each scenario affect the performance of each management strategy.[4]

The IV expansion during the 2020 sell-off was one of the largest and most rapid expansions recorded in the past 20 years, producing historic losses for SPY strangles. Due to the timing and duration of this volatility expansion, 45 DTE contracts opened in February and closed at the end of the March expiration cycle experienced the majority of the expansion and were *especially* affected. Shown in Figure 6.1, the portfolio of contracts held to expiration was immediately wiped out by this extreme market volatility, and the portfolio of early-managed contracts incurred a large drawdown of roughly 40% but ultimately survived. This scenario demonstrates how the loss potential for contracts held to expiration is significantly larger than for contracts managed early. However, this does not

---

[4] Options portfolio backtests should be taken with a grain of salt. Options are highly sensitive to changes in timescale, meaning that a concurrent portfolio with strangles opened on slightly different days, closed on slightly different days, or with slightly different durations may have performed quite differently than the ones shown here.

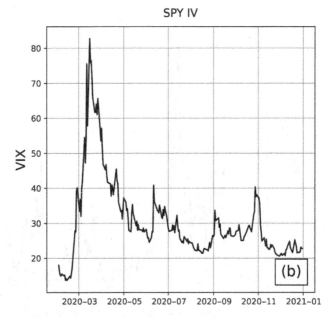

Figure 6.1 (a) Two portfolios, each with $100,000 in capital invested, trading short 45 DTE 16Δ SPY strangles from February 2020 to January 2021. One portfolio consists of strangles managed at 21 DTE (dashed line), and the other consists of strangles held until expiration (solid line). (b) The VIX from February 2020 to January 2021.

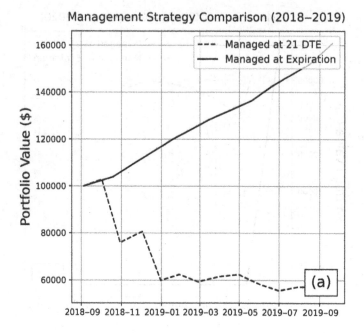

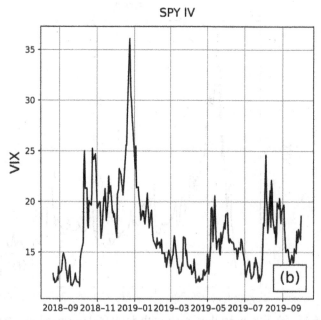

Figure 6.2 (a) Two portfolios, each with $100,000 in capital invested, trading short 45 DTE 16Δ SPY strangles from September 2018 to September 2019. One portfolio consists of strangles managed at 21 DTE (dashed line), and the other consists of strangles held until expiration (solid line). (b) The VIX from September 2018 to September 2019.

necessarily mean that holding to expiration results in more cumulative loss long term.

These same strategies perform quite differently near the end of 2018 when the market experienced smaller, more frequent IV expansions. During this period, the 21 DTE management time for 45 DTE contracts consistently landed on IV peaks during this cycle of market volatility, causing the early-managed portfolio to incur several consecutive losses. Comparatively, the 45 DTE expiration cycles were just long enough to evade these smaller peaks and the portfolio of contracts held to expiration had much stronger performance overall. This scenario demonstrates how having lower per-trade loss potential does not guarantee stronger long-term performance or smaller drawdowns.

Comparing the long-term risks of strategies that occur over different timescales is complicated. These examples show potential trading strategies during unique macroeconomic conditions, but any number of factors could have impacted the realized experience of someone trading during these periods. For instance, if people began trading short 45 DTE 16Δ SPY strangles on February 3, 2020, they would have had a final P/L of −$717 if they managed at 21 DTE and a final P/L of −$8,087 if they held the contract to expiration. If they instead began trading the same strategy *one month later* on March 4, 2020, they would have had a final P/L of −$2,271 if they managed at 21 DTE and a final P/L of $518 if they held the contract to expiration. Strangle risk and performance, particularly during periods of extreme market volatility, are highly sensitive to changes in timescale and IV. There is as much variation in how people choose contract duration, manage positions, and apply stop losses as there are traders. This makes it difficult to model how people *would realistically trade* in a statistically rigorous way and, consequently, creates complications when evaluating the long-term risk of different management strategies.

Rather than factor in long-term risk when selecting a management strategy, the choice should ultimately be based on the following criteria:

- Convenience/consistency.
- Capital allocation preferences and desired number of occurrences.
- Average P/L and outlier loss exposure *per trade*.

Takeaways

1. Traders should choose a *consistent* management strategy to increase the number of occurrences and the chances of achieving favorable long-term averages. Some management strategies include closing a trade at a fixed point in the contract duration, closing a trade at a fixed profit or loss target, or some combination of the two.

2. Compared to trades managed early in the contract duration, trades managed later have larger profits and losses, higher POPs, and allow for fewer occurrences. Early-managed positions accommodate more occurrences and average more P/L per day than positions held to expiration. Closing positions prior to expiration and redeploying capital to new positions is generally a more efficient use of capital compared to extracting more extrinsic value from an existing position.

3. If managing according to DTE, consider closing trades around the contract duration midpoint to achieve a decent amount of long-term profit and justify the tail loss exposure of short premium.

4. To realize reasonable profits and reduce outlier losses, consider a profit threshold between 50% and 75% of the initial credit. A profit or loss target that is too small (say 25% of initial credit) reduces average P/L and per-trade profit potential, and a profit or loss target that is too large does little to mitigate outlier risk.

5. If implementing a stop loss, a mid-range stop loss threshold of at least −200% is practical because there is limited upside potential and still some degree of tail exposure with a very low stop loss.

6. A suitable management strategy depends on an individual's preferences for trade engagement, per-trade average P/L, per-trade outlier risk exposure, and the number of occurrences. Managing undefined risk contracts at 50% of the initial credit or halfway through the contract duration generally achieves reasonable, consistent profits and moderate outlier risk for those more comfortable with active trading. This policy of trading small and trading often also allows for more occurrences.

7. Comparing long-term risks of trade management strategies is complicated because unexpected events, such as the 2020 sell-off, affect short premium strategies differently depending on the contract duration. For this reason, compare the risk and rewards of different strategies on a trade-by-trade basis and choose one based on convenience and consistency, capital allocation preferences, tail exposure preferences, and profit goals.

8. The concepts outlined in this chapter are specific to undefined risk positions. These management principles can also be applied to defined risk positions, but defined risk positions are generally more forgiving because they have limited loss potential. It is not as essential to manage defined risk losses because the maximum loss is known, and in some cases, it may be better to allow a defined risk trade more time to recover rather than close the position at a loss.

Chapter 7

Basic Portfolio Management

Whether adopting an equity, option, or hybrid portfolio, building a portfolio is nontrivial. Identifying a suitable collection of elements, calculating optimal portfolio weights, and maintaining that balance easily becomes hairy. Though countless ways to approach this process exist, the portfolio management tactics discussed in this book are fairly back-of-the-envelope and divided between two chapters. This chapter covers *necessary* guidelines in portfolio management, and the following chapter covers advanced portfolio management including *supplementary* techniques for portfolio optimization. Basic portfolio management includes the following concepts:

- Capital allocation guidelines
- Diversification
- Maintaining portfolio Greeks

Capital Allocation and Position Sizing

The purpose of the dynamic allocation guidelines first introduced in Chapter 3 is to limit portfolio tail exposure while also allowing for reasonable long-term growth by scaling capital allocation according to the current risks and opportunities in the market. Recall that the amount of portfolio buying power allotted to short premium positions, such as short strangles and short iron condors, should range from 25% to 50%, depending on the current market volatility, with the remaining capital either kept in cash or a low-risk passive investment. Of the amount allocated to short premium, at least 75% should be reserved for undefined risk trades (with less than 7% of portfolio buying power allocated to a single position) and at most 25% reserved for defined risk strategies (with less than 5% of portfolio buying power allocated to a single position), although there are exceptions for high probability of profit (POP), defined risk strategies. It's worth mentioning that it is not always feasible to strictly abide by the position size caps of 5% to 7%. If a portfolio has only $10,000 in buying power and implied volatility (IV) is low (i.e., VIX<15), this rule limits the maximum per-trade buying power reduction (BPR) to $700 for an undefined risk trade at a time when BPRs tend to be high. This guideline would severely limit the opportunities available for small accounts. Though total portfolio allocation guidelines *must* be followed, there is more leniency for the per-trade allocation guidelines in smaller accounts.

These guidelines limit the amount of capital exposed to outlier losses, but how capital is allocated depends on personal profit goals and loss tolerances. An options portfolio is typically composed of two types of positions: core and supplemental. Core positions are usually high-POP trades with moderate profit and loss (P/L) standard deviation. These types of positions should offer consistent, fairly reliable profits and reasonable outlier exposure although they will vary by risk tolerance. Consider the following examples:

- Riskier core position: a 45 days to expiration (DTE) 20Δ strangle (undefined risk trade) with a diversified exchange-traded fund (ETF) underlying, such as SPY or QQQ.
- More conservative core position: a 45 DTE 16Δ SPY iron condor with 6Δ wings (high-POP, defined risk trade) with a diversified ETF underlying, such as SPY or QQQ.

Core positions should comprise the majority of a portfolio and be diversified across sectors to develop more reliable portfolio profit and loss expectations and resilience to market volatility. Supplemental positions are not necessarily dependable sources of profit but rather tools for market engagement. These positions are typically higher-risk, higher-reward trades meant to capitalize on dynamic opportunities in the market. Some examples of supplemental positions include earnings trades (which will be discussed in more detail in Chapter 9) or strangles with stock underlyings, such as a 45 DTE 16Δ AAPL strangle. When trading stock underlyings, defined risk supplemental positions would be suitable for more risk-averse traders. These types of positions have significantly more P/L variability than positions with ETF underlyings, resulting in more per-trade profit potential and more loss potential with less dependable profit and loss expectations.

The expected returns, P/L variability, and tail exposure of a portfolio overall primarily depend on the types of core positions, types of supplemental positions, and the ratio of core positions to supplemental positions. Portfolios for more risk-tolerant traders may include a larger percentage of supplemental positions. However, mitigating tail risk remains the highest priority, particularly if the portfolio underlyings are not diversified well. This is why, generally speaking, at most 25% of the capital allocated to short premium should go toward supplemental positions. For example, if the VIX is valued at 45 and 50% of portfolio buying power is allotted to short premium positions (per the allocation guidelines), then at most 25% of the 50% portfolio buying power (or 12.5%) should be allocated to supplemental positions. See Table 7.1 for some numerical context.

Compared to core positions, such as SPY or QQQ strangles, the supplemental positions above have significantly more profit potential, loss potential, and tail risk exposure. The average profit is larger partially as the result of supplemental underlying assets having higher per share prices. This was the case with GOOGL and AMZN, which cost more than the other equity underlyings throughout the entire backtest period. However, these instruments also carry larger profit potentials as option underlyings because they are subject to company-specific risk factors that often inflate the values of their respective options. This was particularly

Table 7.1   Statistics for 45 DTE 16Δ strangles from 2011–2020, managed at expiration. Included are examples for core and supplemental position underlyings.

	Underlying	POP	Average Profit	Average Loss	Conditional Value at Risk (CVaR) (5%)
				16Δ Strangle Statistics (2011–2020)	
	SLV	84%	$32	−$88	−$201
Core	QQQ	74%	$109	−$183	−$454
	SPY	80%	$162	−$320	−$800
	GLD	81%	$119	−$456	−$1,100
	AAPL	74%	$425	−$1,443	−$4,771
Supplemental	GOOGL	80%	$1,174	−$2,955	−$6,593
	AMZN	77%	$1,235	−$2,513	−$6,810

These statistics do not account for IV or stock-specific factors, such as earnings or dividends.

the case with AAPL, which had a *lower* per share value than SPY, QQQ, and GLD throughout this backtest period but more option volatility.

Due to these single-stock risk factors and the variance reflected in the option P/Ls, stocks are generally unsuitable underlyings for core positions. Their high profit potentials make them appealing supplemental position underlyings for opportunistic investors, but mitigating the tail risk exposure from supplemental positions is key for portfolio longevity. The most effective way to accomplish this is by strictly limiting the portfolio capital allocated to high-risk positions.

To summarize, core positions should provide somewhat reliable expectations around P/L and be diversified across sectors. Supplemental positions should comprise a smaller percent of a portfolio because they bring higher profit potentials but also more risk. Diversification, particularly when trading options, is another crucial risk management strategy that can significantly reduce portfolio P/L variability and outlier exposure.

The Basics of Diversification

All financial instruments are subject to some degree of risk, with the risk profiles of some instruments being more flexible than others. A single equity has an immutable risk profile, and an option's risk profile can be adjusted according to multiple parameters. However in either scenario, traders are subject to the risk factors of the particular position. When trading a *portfolio* of assets, a trader may offset the risks of individual positions using complementary positions. Spreading portfolio capital across a variety of assets is known as diversification.

Risk is divided into two broad categories: idiosyncratic and systemic. Idiosyncratic risk is specific to an individual asset, sector, or position and can be minimized using diversification. For example, a portfolio containing only Apple stock is subject to risk factors specific to Apple and the tech sector. Some of those risks can be offset with the addition of an uncorrelated or inversely correlated asset, such as a commodity ETF like GLD. In this more diversified scenario, some hypothetical company-specific risk factors causing AAPL stock to depreciate may be reduced by the performance of GLD, which has relatively independent dynamics.

Comparatively, systemic risk is inherent to the market as a whole and cannot be diversified away. All traded assets are subject to systemic risk because every economy, market, sector, and company has the potential to fail. No amount of diversification will ever remove that element of uncertainty. Instead, the purpose of diversification is to construct a robust portfolio with minimal sensitivity to company-, sector-, or market-specific risk factors.

The process of building a diversified portfolio depends on the types of assets comprising the target portfolio. For an equity portfolio, the most effective way to diversify against idiosyncratic risk is to distribute portfolio capital across assets that have low or inversely correlated price movements. This is because the primary concern when trading equities is the directional movement of the underlying, specifically to the downside. Diversifying portfolio assets, typically using instruments for a variety of companies, sectors, and markets, reduces some of this directional concentration and improves the stability of the portfolio.

To understand the effectiveness of diversification by this method, consider the example outlined next. Table 7.2 shows different portfolio allocation percentages for two equity portfolios, Table 7.3 shows the correlation of the assets in both portfolios, and Figure 7.1 shows the comparative performance of the two portfolios. The historical directional tendencies are often estimated using the correlation coefficient, which quantifies the strength of the historical linear relationship between two variables. Recall that the correlation coefficient ranges from −1 to 1, with 1 corresponding to perfect positive correlation, −1 corresponding to perfect inverse correlation, and 0 corresponding to no measured correlation.

Table 7.2   Two sample portfolios, each containing some percentage of market ETFs for reliable portfolio growth (SPY, QQQ), low volatility assets for diversification (GLD, TLT), and high volatility assets for increased profit potential (AMZN, AAPL).

	% Portfolio Allocation	
	Portfolio A	Portfolio B
Market ETFs	40%	50%
Low Volatility Assets	50%	0
High Volatility Assets	10%	50%

These portfolio weights were determined intuitively and not by any particular quantitative methodology. This example demonstrates the effectiveness of diversification rather than providing a specific framework for achieving diversification in equity portfolios.

Table 7.3   The five-year correlation history for the assets in Portfolios A and B. Though these relationships fluctuate with time over short timescales, they are assumed to remain relatively constant long term.

		Correlation (2015–2020)					
		SPY	QQQ	GLD	TLT	AMZN	AAPL
Market	SPY	1.0	0.89	−0.13	−0.33	0.62	0.64
ETFs	QQQ	0.89	1.0	−0.12	−0.26	0.75	0.74
Low Volatility	GLD	−0.13	−0.12	1.0	0.39	−0.12	−0.11
Assets	TLT	−0.33	−0.26	0.39	1.0	−0.18	−0.22
High Volatility	AMZN	0.62	0.75	−0.12	−0.18	1.0	0.50
Assets	AAPL	0.64	0.74	−0.11	−0.22	0.50	1.0

Table 7.2 outlines two portfolios: Portfolio A is a relatively diversified portfolio with conservative risk tolerances and moderate profit expectations, while Portfolio B is a risk tolerant and fairly concentrated portfolio. Table 7.3 shows how the elements in Portfolio B (SPY, QQQ, AMZN, AAPL) have fairly high mutual historic correlations and therefore similar

directional tendencies. Comparatively, half of Portfolio A is allocated to low volatility assets that are uncorrelated or inversely correlated with the market ETFs and high volatility assets. Therefore, due to the diversifying contributions of those relatively independent assets, Portfolio A is less sensitive to outlier market events. Figure 7.1 shows how these portfolios would have performed from 2020–2021, importantly including the 2020 sell-off and subsequent recovery.

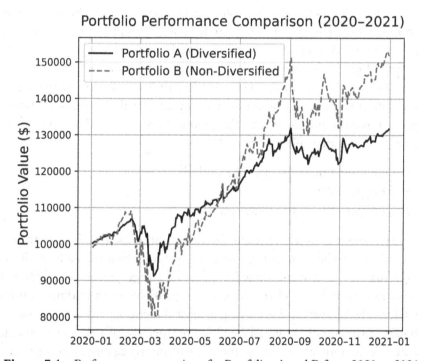

Figure 7.1   Performance comparison for Portfolios A and B from 2020 to 2021. Each portfolio begins with $100,000 in initial capital.

Historic correlations have become *stronger* during financial crashes and sell-offs. Stated differently, assets have become more correlated or more inversely correlated during volatile market periods. The correlations in Table 7.2, therefore, *underestimate* the correlation magnitudes that would have been measured from 2020–2021.

As a result of the COVID-19 pandemic, market ETFs and highly correlated assets, such as large cap tech stocks incurred significant drawdowns. Portfolio B, half of which was high volatile tech stocks, crashed by roughly 25% from February to late March 2020. Comparatively,

Portfolio A still experienced massive drawdowns but only declined by 14% during the same period. Portfolio B is significantly more exposed to market volatility than Portfolio A, resulting in a more rapid, but unstable recovery following the 2020 sell-off. Throughout this year, Portfolio B grew by roughly 90% from its minimum in March while Portfolio A was growing by 44%, but Portfolio B was nearly twice as volatile. Nondiversified portfolios are generally more sensitive to sector- or market-specific fluctuations compared to diversified portfolios. Diversifying a portfolio across asset classes reduces position concentration risk and tends to reduce loss potential in the event of turbulent market conditions. However, Figure 7.1 shows how more volatile, higher-risk portfolios can pay off with higher profits.

Due to their complex risk profiles, options are inherently more diversified relative to one another compared to their equity counterparts. Unlike equities, where the primary concern is directional risk, several factors may affect option P/L:

- Directional movement in the underlying price.
- Changes in IV.
- Changes in time to expiration.

Because exposure to each of these variables can be controlled according to the contract parameters, varying factors, such as duration/management time, underlying, and strategy creates an additional reduction in P/L correlation that is not possible when trading equities exclusively. However, diversifying against directional risk of the underlyings remains most essential from the perspective of risk management, particularly outlier risk management. Diversifying against nondirectional risk by varying strategy or contract duration is supplemental.

To understand why it is so essential to diversify the option underlyings of a portfolio, consider two market ETFs: SPY and QQQ. These assets have historically had highly correlated price dynamics and IV dynamics, as shown in the correlation matrix in Table 7.4.

The equity underlyings and IV indices are highly correlated, meaning that IV expansion events and outlier price moves tend to happen

Table 7.4 Historic correlations between two market ETFs (SPY, QQQ) and the correlations between their implied volatility indices (VIX, VXN) from 2011 to 2020. Also included is the correlation between each market index and the respective VIX, for reference.

		Equity Price and IV Index Correlation (2011–2020)			
		SPY	QQQ	VIX	VXN
Equities	SPY	1.0	0.89	−0.80	
	QQQ	0.89	1.0		−0.76
Volatility	VIX	−0.80		1.0	0.89
Indices	VXN		−0.76	0.89	1.0

simultaneously for these two assets. When such events do occur, short premium positions with these two underlyings may experience simultaneous tail losses. To get an idea of how often these positions have incurred simultaneous outlier losses historically, refer to the strangle statistics shown in Table 7.5.

Table 7.5 The probability of outlier losses (worse than 200% of the initial credit) occurring simultaneously for 16Δ SPY strangles and 16Δ QQQ strangles from 2011 to 2020. All contracts have approximately the same duration (45 DTE), start date, and expiration date. The diagonal entries (SPY Strangle-SPY Strangle, QQQ Strangle-QQQ Strangle) indicate the probability of a strategy incurring an outlier loss individually, and the off-diagonal entries correspond to the probability of the pair incurring outlier losses simultaneously.

	Probability of Loss Worse than 200% (2011–2020)	
	SPY Strangle	QQQ Strangle
SPY Strangle	5.8%	3.9%
QQQ Strangle	3.9%	8.7%

Table 7.5 shows that it is reasonably unlikely for the pair of strategies to incur outlier losses simultaneously having occurred only 3.9% of

the time. However, if these events were completely independent, then these compound losses would have occurred less than 1% of the time: $5.8\% \times 8.7\% \approx 0.50\%$. Additionally, when considering the outlier loss probability for each strategy on an individual basis, the effects of trading strangles with correlated underlyings becomes a bit clearer.

For example, the probability of a SPY strangle incurring an outlier loss is 5.8%. What is the probability a QQQ strangle will incur a simultaneous outlier loss given that a SPY strangle has taken an outlier loss? To calculate this, one can use conditional probability.[1]

$$P(\text{QQQ loss given SPY loss}) = \frac{P\,(\text{SPY loss and QQQ loss})}{P(\text{SPY loss})}$$

$$= \frac{3.9\%}{5.8\%} \approx 67\%$$

In other words, SPY strangles and QQQ strangles may only have simultaneous outlier losses 3.9% of the time, but when a SPY strangle incurs an outlier loss, there is a *67% chance* that a QQQ strangle also will.[2] Generally, the probability of a compound loss is fairly low, but when one short premium position takes a loss there is often a high likelihood an equivalent position with a correlated underlying will experience a loss of comparable magnitude. Because the loss potential of these compound occurrences is so large, it is essential to diversify underlying equities and maintain appropriate position sizes for correlated options to reduce the likelihood and impact of compounding outlier losses.

Now consider two market ETFs (SPY and QQQ) and two diversifying ETFs that have been uncorrelated or inversely correlated to the market (GLD, TLT). The historic correlations are shown in Table 7.6 and the probability of outlier losses occurring simultaneously are shown in Table 7.7.

---

[1] For an introduction to conditional probability, refer to the appendix.
[2] A 67% conditional probability of a compound loss is very high but lower than the compound loss probability when trading the equivalent equities. SPY and QQQ are *highly* correlated and experience near-identical drawdowns in periods of market turbulence. Therefore, that these options incur compound outlier losses only 70% of the time demonstrates the inherent diversification of options alluded to earlier.

Table 7.6 Historic correlations among two market ETFs (SPY and QQQ), a gold ETF (GLD), and a bond ETF (TLT) from 2011 to 2020.

Equity Price Correlation (2011–2020)

	SPY	QQQ	GLD	TLT
SPY	1.0	0.89	−0.03	−0.41
QQQ	0.89	1.0	−0.04	−0.34
GLD	−0.03	−0.04	1.0	0.23
TLT	−0.41	−0.34	0.23	1.0

Table 7.7 The probability of outlier losses (worse than 200% of the initial credit) occurring simultaneously for different types of 16Δ strangles held to expiration from 2011 to 2020. All contracts have approximately the same duration (45 DTE), open and close dates. The diagonal entries correspond to the probability of the specific strategy incurring an outlier loss individually, and the off-diagonal entries correspond to the probability of the pair incurring outlier losses simultaneously.

Probability of Loss Worse than 200% for Different Strangles (2011–2020)

	SPY	QQQ	GLD	TLT
SPY	5.8%	3.9%	2.1%	1.9%
QQQ	3.9%	8.7%	1.9%	1.7%
GLD	2.1%	1.9%	12%	4.8%
TLT	1.9%	1.7%	4.8%	12%

Again, it is relatively unlikely for any pair to incur simultaneous outlier losses, but this table shows the significant reduction in the *conditional* outlier probability when the underlying assets are uncorrelated or inversely correlated. Consider the following:

- If a SPY strangle incurs an outlier loss, there is a 67% chance of a compounding loss with a QQQ strangle.
- If a SPY strangle incurs an outlier loss, there is a 36% chance of a compounding loss with a GLD strangle.
- If a QQQ strangle incurs an outlier loss, there is a 20% chance of a compounding loss with a TLT strangle.

Compound losses still occur when the underlying assets have low or inversely correlated price movements, but this reduction in likelihood is crucial nonetheless. Having a portfolio that includes uncorrelated or inversely correlated assets is particularly meaningful during periods of unexpected market volatility when most assets develop a stronger correlation to the market and there are widespread expansions in IV. Though options can be diversified with respect to several variables, diversifying the underlying assets is one of the most effective ways to reduce the impact of outlier events on a portfolio. Because diversification does not entirely remove the risk of compounding outlier losses, so maintaining small position sizes (at most 5% to 7% of portfolio capital allocated to a single position) remains critical.

Maintaining Portfolio Greeks

The Greeks form a set of risk measures that quantify different dimensions of exposure for options. Each contract has its own specific set of Greeks, but some Greeks have the convenient property of being additive across positions with different underlyings. Consequently, these metrics can be used to summarize the various sources of risk for a portfolio and guide adjustments. The following portfolio Greeks will be the focus of this section:

- Beta-weighted delta ($\beta\Delta$): Recall from Chapter 1 that beta is a measure of systematic risk and specifically quantifies the directional tendency of the stock relative to that of the overall market. Stocks with positive correlation to the market have positive beta and stocks with negative correlation have negative beta. $\beta\Delta$ is similar to delta, which is the expected change in the option price given a $1 change in the price of the underlying. When delta is beta-weighted, the adjusted value corresponds to the expected change in the option price given a $1 change in some reference index, such as SPY.
- Theta (θ): The decline in an option's value due to the passage of time, all else being equal. This is generally represented as the expected decrease in an option's value per day.

Maintaining the balance of these two variables is crucial for the long-term health of a short options portfolio. $\beta\Delta$ represents the amount of directional exposure a position has relative to some index rather than the underlying itself. The cumulative portfolio $\beta\Delta$ delta represents the overall directional exposure of the portfolio relative to the market assuming that the beta index is a market ETF like SPY. Normalizing delta according to a standard underlying allows delta to be additive across all portfolio positions. This *cannot* be done with unweighted delta because $1 moves across different underlyings are not comparable, i.e., trying to add deltas of different positions is like adding inches and ounces. For example, a 50Δ sensitivity to underlying A and a 25Δ sensitivity to underlying B does not imply a 75Δ sensitivity to anything, unless A and B happen to be perfectly correlated.

$\beta\Delta$ neutral portfolios are attractive to short premium traders because the portfolio is relatively insensitive to changes in the market, and profit is primarily driven by changes in IV and time. Adopting $\beta\Delta$ neutrality also simplifies aspects of the diversification process because a near-zero $\beta\Delta$ indicates low directional market exposure. As the delta of a position drifts throughout the contract duration, the overall delta of the portfolio is skewed. To maintain $\beta\Delta$ neutrality, existing positions can be re-centered (where the current trade is closed and reopened with a new delta), existing positions can be closed entirely, or new positions can be added. The most appropriate strategy depends on the current portfolio theta.

Theta is also additive across positions because the units of theta are identical for all options ($/day). Because short premium traders consistently profit from time decay, the total theta across positions gives a reliable estimate for the expected daily growth of the portfolio. The theta ratio (theta/net portfolio liquidity) estimates the expected daily profit per unit of capital for a short premium portfolio. Options portfolios are subject to significant tail risk, so the expected daily profit should be significantly higher than a portfolio passively invested in the market to justify that risk. Therefore, one can determine the benchmark profit goals of an equivalent short options portfolio by referring to the daily P/L performance of a passively invested SPY portfolio as shown below in Table 7.8.

Table 7.8 Daily performance statistics for five portfolios passively invested in SPY from 2011–2021. Each portfolio has $100,000 in initial capital, and the amount of capital allocated in each portfolio ranges from 25% to 50%.

SPY Allocation Percentage	Daily Portfolio P/L (2011–2021)
25%	0.013%
30%	0.015%
35%	0.017%
40%	0.020%
50%	0.025%

From 2011–2021, a passively invested SPY portfolio collected between 0.013% and 0.025% daily depending on the percentage of capital allocated. In other words, these portfolios had daily profits between $13 and $25 per $100,000 of capital over the past 10 years ($100,000 × 0.00013). However, the expected daily profit per unit of capital for a short options portfolio should be *significantly* higher than this benchmark. For most traders, the minimum theta ratio should range from 0.05% to 0.1% of portfolio net liquidity to justify the tail risks of short premium. In other words, short premium portfolios should have a daily expected profit between $50 and $100 per $100,000 of portfolio buying power from theta decay.

The theta ratio should not exceed 0.2%. A higher theta ratio is preferable, but it should not be too high due to hidden gamma risk. Gamma (Γ) is the expected change in the option's delta given a $1 change in the price of the underlying. Delta neutral positions are rarely gamma neutral, and if the gamma of a position is especially high, then the delta of the trade is highly sensitive to changes in the underlying price and is generally unstable. A position with high delta sensitivity can easily affect the overall $\beta\Delta$ neutrality of a portfolio.

The gammas of different derivatives cannot be compared across underlyings for similar reasons as to why raw delta cannot be compared across underlyings. Gamma cannot be accurately beta-weighted as delta can; however, a positive relationship between gamma and theta presents a solution to this problem. Positions with large amounts of theta, such as trades with strikes that are close to at-the-money (ATM) or trades that are near expiration, typically also have large amounts of gamma risk. Because theta is additive across portfolio positions, the theta ratio is the most direct indicator of excessive gamma risk. This relationship between gamma and theta also demonstrates how short premium traders must balance the profitability of time decay with the P/L fluctuations resulting from gamma.

To summarize, the theta ratio for an options portfolio should range from 0.05% to 0.1% and should not exceed 0.2%. Based on the theta ratio and the amount of capital currently allocated, existing positions should then be re-centered, short premium positions should be added, or short premium positions should be removed. Given these benchmarks for expected daily profits, the procedure for modifying portfolio positions can be summarized as follows:

- If a properly allocated, a well-diversified portfolio is $\beta\Delta$ neutral but does not provide a sufficient amount of theta, then the positions in the portfolio should be reevaluated. In this case, perhaps some defined risk trades should be replaced with undefined risk trades or undefined risk positions should be rolled to higher deltas. New delta neutral positions can also be added, such as strangles and iron condors, for example. IV and theta are also highly correlated, meaning that higher IV underlyings could also be considered if theta is too low. These measures can be reversed if the portfolio has too much theta exposure while being $\beta\Delta$ neutral.
- If the theta ratio is too low (<0.1%), then either existing positions should be re-centered/tightened or new short premium positions should be added.
  - If the $\beta\Delta$ is too large and positive (bullish), then add new negative $\beta\Delta$ positions (e.g., add short calls on positive beta underlyings or add short puts on negative beta underlyings).
  - If the $\beta\Delta$ is too large and negative (bearish), then add new positive $\beta\Delta$ positions (e.g., add short puts on positive beta underlyings).
- If the theta ratio is too large (>0.2%), then either existing positions should be re-centered/widened or short premium positions should be removed.
  - If the $\beta\Delta$ is too large and positive (bullish), then remove positive $\beta\Delta$ positions (e.g., remove short puts on positive beta underlyings).
  - If the $\beta\Delta$ is too large and negative (bearish), then remove negative $\beta\Delta$ positions (e.g., remove short calls on positive beta underlyings).

- If a properly allocated, well-diversified portfolio provides a sufficient amount of theta but is not $\beta\Delta$ neutral, then existing positions should be reevaluated. For example, skewed positions could be closed and re-centered or replaced with new delta-neutral positions that offer comparable amounts of theta.

Takeaways

1. The amount of portfolio buying power allotted to short premium positions should range from 25% to 50% depending on the current market volatility, with the remaining capital either kept in cash or a low-risk passive investment. Of the amount allocated, at least 75% should be reserved for undefined risk trades (with no more than 7% allocated to a single position), and at most 25% should be reserved for defined risk strategies (with no more than 5% allocated to a single position). The total portfolio allocation guidelines *must* be followed, but there is more leniency for the per-trade allocation guidelines, especially in smaller accounts.
2. An options portfolio is typically composed of two types of positions: core and supplemental. Core positions are usually high-POP trades with moderate P/L variance that offer consistent profits and reasonable outlier exposure. Supplemental positions are not necessarily dependable sources of profit but rather tools for market engagement. At most 25% of the capital allocated to short premium should go toward supplemental positions.
3. Unlike equity portfolios, options portfolios can be diversified with respect to multiple variables, such as duration/management time, underlying, and strategy. Diversifying the underlyings of an options portfolio remains the most essential diversification tool for portfolio risk management, particularly outlier risk management.
4. Beta-weighted delta ($\beta\Delta$) represents the amount of directional exposure a position has relative to some index rather than the underlying itself. Portfolio theta (θ) represents the expected daily growth of the portfolio. The minimum theta ratio for an options portfolio should range from 0.05% to 0.1% and should not exceed 0.2%. Maintaining the balance of these two Greeks ensures the risk-reward profile of an options portfolio remains as close to the target as possible.

Chapter 8

Advanced Portfolio Management

Having covered the necessary basics of portfolio management, this chapter discusses supplemental optimization techniques for traders who can accommodate more active trading. The capital allocation guidelines, underlying diversification, and Greeks of a portfolio are essential to maintain and are relatively straightforward to employ. This chapter will introduce some less essential strategies:

- Additional option diversification techniques.
- Weighting assets according to probability of profit (POP).

Advanced Diversification

As stated in the previous chapter, one of the biggest strategic differences between equity portfolios and options portfolios is the ability to diversify risk with respect to factors other than price. Diversifying with respect to the underlying is the most effective way to reduce the effect of outlier events on a portfolio. Diversifying with respect to other variables, such as time and strategy, requires more active management but tends to reduce the profit and loss (P/L) correlation between positions. For example, consider the per-day standard deviation of P/L for SPY strangles with different durations as shown in Figure 8.1.

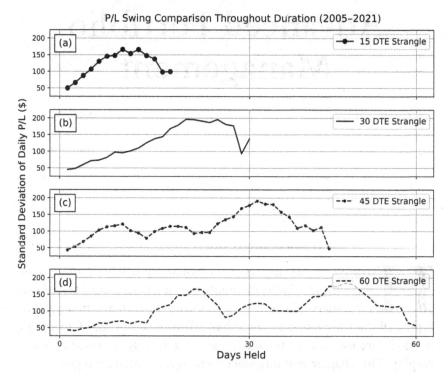

Figure 8.1 Standard deviation of daily P/Ls (in dollars) for 16Δ SPY strangles with various durations from 2005–2021. Included are durations of (a) 15 days to expiration (DTE), (b) 30 DTE, (c) 45 DTE, and (d) 60 DTE.

Short premium trades tend to have more volatile P/L swings as they approach expiration, a result of the position becoming more sensitive to changes in time and underlying price (larger gamma and theta). Because contracts with different durations have varying sensitivities to these factors at a given time, diversifying the timescales of portfolio positions reduces the correlations among their P/L dynamics. Because trading consistent contract durations is important for reaching many occurrences, the most effective way to diversify with respect to time is by trading contracts with consistent durations but a variety of expiration dates. This strategy achieves an assortment of contract durations in a portfolio at a given time without compromising the number of occurrences. Despite its efficacy, diversification with respect to time will not be thoroughly covered in this chapter because it is difficult to maintain conveniently and consistently.

Strategy diversification, while not as essential as underlying diversification, is another risk management technique that is more straightforward than time diversification. This method effectively spreads portfolio capital across different risk profiles while maintaining the same directional assumption for a given underlying (or a highly correlated underlying). This lets traders capitalize on the directional dynamics of an asset while protecting a proportion of portfolio capital from outlier losses. To see an example of the diversification potential for this method, consider a backtest of three different portfolios. Each portfolio contains some combination of two directionally neutral SPY strategies: strangles and iron condors. The performance of these portfolios in this long-term backtest is shown in Figure 8.2 and analyzed in Table 8.1. The purpose of this backtest is not to demonstrate the profit or loss potential associated with combining SPY strangles and iron condors but rather to illustrate the possible effects of strategy diversification on portfolio risk according to one sample of outcomes.

The impact of diversification is immediately clear, particularly when emphasizing the drawdowns of the 2020 sell-off. Strangles and iron condors experienced massive drawdowns in early 2020 even though defined risk trades are lower-risk, lower-reward trades. The cumulative drawdowns as a percentage of portfolio capital are approximately the same across all three portfolios (roughly 150%). However, the drawdowns as a raw dollar amount were significantly larger for the strangle portfolio compared to the combined portfolio. During more regular market conditions, the combined portfolio also had a much larger POP and profit potential than the iron condor portfolio and less P/L variability and outlier risk than the strangle portfolio.

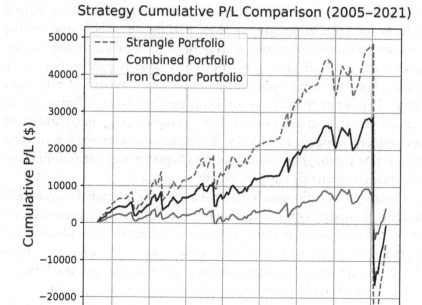

Figure 8.2 Cumulative P/L of three different portfolios containing some combination of SPY strangles and SPY iron condors, held to expiration from 2005–2021. The strangle portfolio contains 10 strangles, the combined portfolio contains five strangles and five iron condors, and the iron condor portfolio contains 10 iron condors. All contracts are traded once per expiration cycle, opened at the beginning of the expiration cycle and closed at expiration. These positions have the same short delta (16Δ), approximately the same duration (45 DTE), and the same open and close dates. The long strikes of the iron condors are roughly 10Δ.

This example demonstrates how diversifying portfolio capital across defined and undefined risk strategies lets a trader capitalize on the directional tendencies of an underlying asset (or several highly correlated underlyings) while protecting a fraction of capital from unlikely outlier events. However, this example combines strategies in a highly simplified way as market implied volatility (IV), capital allocation guidelines, alternative management techniques, and strategy-specific factors are

Table 8.1 Statistical analysis of the three portfolios illustrated in Figure 8.2. The first four statistics (POP, average P/L, standard deviation of P/L, and conditional value at risk (CVaR)) gauge portfolio performance during more regular market conditions (2005–2020). The final column gives the worst-case drawdown from the 2020 sell-off (the cumulative losses from February to March 2020).

Portfolio Type	2005–2020				2020 Sell-Off
	POP	Average P/L	Standard Deviation of P/L	CVaR (5%)	Worst-Case Drawdowns
Strangle	76%	$379	$1,803	−$5,174	−$77,520
Combined	75%	$221	$1,275	−$3,648	−$45,080
Iron Condor	67%	$64	$799	−$2,324	−$12,640

not considered. In practice, defined and undefined risk strategies reach P/L targets at different rates and often require different management strategies. The percentage of capital allocated to a single position also depends on a number of factors, including the buying power reduction (BPR) of the trade (maximum of 5% for defined risk trades and 7% for undefined risk) and the correlation with the existing positions in a portfolio. For traders interested in a more quantitative approach to positional capital allocation, allocation weights can be estimated from the probability of profit of the strategy.

Balancing Capital According to POP

The proportion of capital to allocate to a position can be estimated from the POP of the strategy. An appropriate percentage of buying power can be estimated using the following formula, derived from the Kelly Criterion:[1]

$$f = r \cdot \frac{\text{DTE}}{365} \cdot \frac{\text{POP}}{1 - \text{POP}} \qquad (8.1)$$

where r is the annualized risk-free rate of return, DTE is days to expiration or the contract duration (in calendar days), and POP is the

[1] For an introduction to the Kelly Criterion, refer to the appendix.

probability of profit of the strategy.[2] Approximating the risk-free rate is not straightforward because it is an unobservable market-wide constant, but the long-term bond rate is commonly used as a conservative estimate. For the remainder of this chapter, the risk-free rate will be estimated at roughly 3% for the sake of simplicity. To see some examples of portfolio allocation percentages calculated using this equation, see Table 8.2.

Table 8.2   POPs and allocation percentages of buying power for 45 DTE 16Δ SPY, QQQ, and GLD strangles from 2011–2018.

	Strangle Statistics (2011–2018)	
	POP	Allocation Percentages
SPY Strangle	79%	1.4%
QQQ Strangle	73%	1.0%
GLD Strangle	84%	1.9%

The equation above suggests that the amount of portfolio buying power allocated to these positions should range from 1.0% to 1.9%, but those calculations don't take correlations between positions into account. Strategies with perfectly correlated underlyings should be counted against the same percentage of portfolio capital because Equation (8.1) requires that trades be independent of one another. In this example, because SPY and QQQ are highly correlated to each other but mutually uncorrelated with GLD, GLD strangles can occupy an entire 1.9% of portfolio buying power, and SPY strangles and QQQ strangles *combined* should occupy around 1.4% (the larger of the two allocation percentages). Because SPY and QQQ are not perfectly correlated, this is a conservative lower bound.

Overall, these allocation percentages are fairly low because the Kelly Criterion advocates for placing many small, uncorrelated bets. When aiming to allocate between 25% and 50% of portfolio buying power, strictly abiding by these bet sizes is somewhat impractical; there just aren't enough uncorrelated underlyings. The value of the risk-free rate

---

[2] The POPs used throughout this chapter are calculated from historic options data. Options data are ideal for statistical analyses but inaccessible to most people. Trading platforms often provide the theoretical POP of a strategy, which can substitute measured POP for these calculations.

provides a *conservative* estimate for the ideal capital allocation, so scaling these percentages up and adopting a more aggressive approach is justified. To scale up these percentages without violating the capital allocation guidelines, these bet sizes can be used as a heuristic to estimate *proportions* of capital allocation rather than the explicit percentages. For example, rather than allocating according to POP weights, a more heuristic approach would be as follows:

- According to initial estimates, 1.4% of portfolio buying power should be allocated to SPY strangles and 1.9% to GLD strangles.
- Dividing by 1.9, these weights correspond to a ratio of approximately 0.74:1.0.
- This means that SPY strangles should occupy roughly 0.74 times the portfolio buying power of GLD strangles.
- If the maximum per-trade allocation of 7% goes toward GLD strangles, then approximately 5.2% (derived from $0.74 \times 7\% = 5.2\%$) should be allocated to SPY strangles.

To continue this example, suppose that the capital allocated to SPY strangles is further split between SPY strangles and QQQ strangles. Although these underlyings are correlated, splitting capital between these positions achieves more diversification than allocating the entire 5.2% to one underlying. This process can also be estimated using the POP weights:

- According to initial estimates, 1.4% of portfolio buying power should be allocated to SPY strangles and 1.0% to QQQ strangles.
- Dividing by 2.4% (from 1.4% + 1.0%), these weights correspond to a ratio of approximately 0.58:0.42.
- This means that SPY strangles should occupy 58% of the capital allocation and QQQ strangles should occupy 42%.
- If a maximum of 5.2% can be allocated toward these positions, then 3.0% of portfolio capital should go toward SPY strangles and 2.2% to QQQ strangles.

This scaling formula, when combined with position sizing caps of the capital allocation guidelines, allows traders to construct portfolio weights that scale with the POP of a strategy without overexposing capital to outlier risk. These two concepts form a simple but effective basis for options portfolio construction.

Constructing a Sample Portfolio

Throughout this section, simplified capital allocation guidelines, option diversification, and POP-weighting are combined to create a sample portfolio. The sample portfolio shown here will be constructed using data from January 2011 to January 01, 2018 and backtested with data from January 02, 2018 to September 2019. This backtest will focus on implementing some of the portfolio construction techniques outlined in Chapters 7 and 8. This sample portfolio has six different core positions (all strangles), each occupying a constant amount of portfolio capital determined by the POP-weight scaling method described in the previous section. The following three simplifications are made for ease of analysis and understanding:

1. Neither market IV nor underlying IV will be considered. Scaling portfolio allocation up when market IV increases is an effective way to capitalize on higher premium prices, as is focusing on underlyings with inflated implied volatilities. Because a constant 30% of portfolio capital will be allotted to the same short premium positions throughout this backtest, profit potential will be significantly limited. Therefore, the focus of this analysis is risk management.

2. This study only uses strangles with exchange-traded fund (ETF) underlyings instead of a combination of strategies. This makes the portfolio approximately delta neutral and eliminates the need to justify specific directional assumptions or risk profiles for individual assets. By disregarding stock underlyings, stock-specific binary events, such as earnings and dividends do not apply. This also means that the added profit potential from supplemental positions (which tend to be higher risk and include stock underlyings) will not be accounted for in this backtest.

3. Rather than managing trades at fixed profit targets, all the trades shown in this backtest will be approximately opened on the first of the month and closed at the end of the month.

Step 1: Identify suitable underlyings using past data. Core positions should have moderate P/L standard deviations and well-diversified underlying assets. ETFs, such as the ones in Table 8.3, are viable candidates for core position underlyings. Though the market ETFs are highly correlated, a sufficient number of uncorrelated and inversely correlated assets can achieve a reasonable reduction in idiosyncratic risk.

Table 8.3 Correlations between different ETFs from 2011–2018. Included are two market ETFs (SPY, QQQ), a gold ETF (GLD), a bond ETF (TLT), a currency ETF (FXE - Euro), and a utilities ETF (XLU).

		Correlation (2011–2018)					
		SPY	**QQQ**	**GLD**	**TLT**	**FXE**	**XLU**
Market ETFs	**SPY**	1.0	0.88	−0.02	−0.44	0.16	0.49
	QQQ	0.88	1.0	−0.03	−0.36	0.12	0.35
Diversifying ETFs	**GLD**	−0.02	−0.03	1.0	0.19	0.34	0.08
	TLT	−0.44	−0.36	0.19	1.0	−0.03	−0.04
	FXE	0.16	0.12	0.34	−0.03	1.0	0.18
	XLU	0.49	0.35	0.08	−0.04	0.18	1.0

Step 2: Calculate the percentage of portfolio capital that should be allocated to each position. These percentages can be estimated with Equation (8.1) and scaled according to the methodology described in the previous section, as shown in Table 8.4.

The core positions shown in Table 8.4 are high-POP, have moderate P/L standard deviation, and have well-diversified underlyings, and the allocation amounts are below the 7% per-trade buying power maximum. The total portfolio buying power allocated to short premium amounts to 30%, which is close enough to the minimum 25% to suffice for this backtest. With the portfolio initialized using data from 2011 to early 2018, it can now be backtested on new data from early 2018 to late 2019, bearing in mind that this test does not take dynamic management or implied volatility into account. The results of backtesting this sample portfolio are shown in Figure 8.3 and Table 8.5.[3]

Interestingly, Table 8.5 shows that the equity portfolio was the most volatile of the three and experienced the largest worst-case drawdown despite having less tail exposure than the options portfolios. The POP-weighted portfolio performed more consistently and had

---

[3] This backtest demonstrates one specific outcome out of many possible when trading short premium. The goal of this backtest is to demonstrate how one sample portfolio performs relative to other portfolios with similar characteristics under these specific circumstances.

Table 8.4 Core position statistics for 45 DTE 16Δ strangles from 2011–2018. The allocation ratio is the allocation percentages normalized such that the largest bet size is set to 1.0. The portfolio weights are determined by multiplying the allocation ratio by 7% (the maximum per-trade allocation percentage). The adjusted portfolio weights show how portfolio capital is split across assets that are highly correlated.

	Core Position Statistics (2011–2018)	
	POP	**Allocation Percentages**
SPY Strangle	79%	1.4%
QQQ Strangle	73%	1.0%
GLD Strangle	84%	1.9%
TLT Strangle	78%	1.3%
FXE Strangle	83%	1.8%
XLU Strangle	81%	1.6%
Allocation Ratio	**SPY/QQQ:GLD:TLT:FXE:XLU** 0.74:1.0:0.68:0.95:0.84	
Portfolio Weights	**SPY/QQQ:GLD:TLT:FXE:XLU** 5.2%:7.0%:4.8%:6.7%:5.9%	
Adjusted Portfolio Weights	**SPY:QQQ:GLD:TLT:FXE:XLU** 3.0%:2.2%:7.0%:4.8%:6.7%:5.9%	

significantly less per-trade standard deviation than either of the other two, with per-trade POP matching the equal-weight portfolio and average P/L comparable to the equity portfolio. Despite consisting of undefined risk strategies, the POP-weighted portfolio had nearly half the P/L variability and worst-case loss as the equity portfolio throughout the backtest period. The equal-weight strangle portfolio also under-performed compared to the POP-weighted portfolio although not experiencing any more P/L variance or severe drawdowns compared to a comparable portfolio of equities. To reiterate, the performance of both strangle portfolios can be further optimized by increasing the allocation percentage according to market volatility (which can be done with the addition of uncorrelated short premium positions) or by incorporating more complex management strategies. Still, this simplified backtest illustrates the impact of incorporating the risk management techniques of capital allocation, diversification, and POP-weighted allocation.

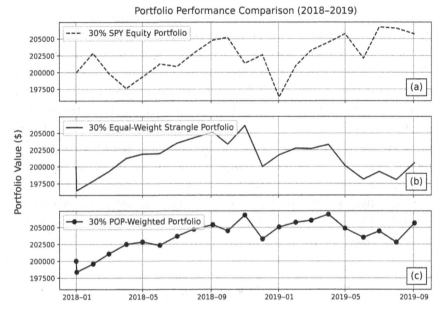

Figure 8.3 Portfolio performance of three different portfolios from early 2018 until September of 2019. Each portfolio has $200,000 in initial capital with 30% of the portfolio capital allocated. This initial amount of $200,000 allows at least one trade for each type of position, as $100,000 in initial capital does not. The 30% SPY equity portfolio (a) has 30% allocated to shares of SPY. The 30% equally-weighted strangle portfolio (b) has 5% allocated to each of the six types of strangles, and the 30% POP-weighted portfolio (c) has the 30% weighted according to the percentages in Table 8.4. All contracts have the same delta (16Δ), identical durations (roughly 45 DTE), and the same open and close dates. For the sake of comparison, the trades in the equity portfolio are opened on the first of each month and closed at the end of each month.

Table 8.5 Portfolio backtest performance statistics for the three portfolios described in Figure 8.3 from 2018–2019.

Portfolio Performance Comparison (2018–2019)

Portfolio Type	POP	Average P/L	Standard Deviation of P/L	Worst Loss
SPY Equity	60%	$285	$2,879	−$6,319
Equal-Weight	67%	$26	$2,440	−$6,117
POP-Weighted	67%	$268	$1,610	−$3,561

The $\frac{POP}{1-POP}$ heuristic derived from the Kelly Criterion provides a good guide for how much capital should be allocated to a trade when initializing a portfolio, indicating that more capital should be allocated to higher POP trades and less capital should be allocated to less reliable trades. However, this method does not provide a thorough structure for dynamic portfolio management. At different points in time, trades often reach profit or loss targets, require strike re-centering, or present new opportunities. Traders can simplify the complex management process by, for example, choosing the same contract duration or management strategy for all trades in a portfolio. However, a framework for navigating these dynamic circumstances is still necessary, and this is where the portfolio Greeks and the re-balancing protocol outlined in Chapter 7 are particularly useful.

Takeaways

1. Options can be diversified with respect to a number of variables, but diversifying the equity underlyings of an options portfolio remains the most essential for portfolio risk management. Traders who can accommodate more involvement and are interested in further diversification can also diversify positions with respect to time and strategy.

2. Diversification with respect to time tends to reduce the correlations between portfolio positions because contracts respond differently to changes in time, volatility, and underlying price depending on their duration. The most effective way to diversify with respect to time without compromising occurrences is by trading contracts with consistent durations but a variety of expiration dates. This strategy is difficult to maintain consistently, however, particularly when multiple management strategies are used.

3. Diversifying portfolio capital across defined and undefined risk strategies allows traders to capitalize on the directional tendencies of an underlying asset while protecting a fraction of capital from unlikely outlier events. If implementing this diversification technique, note that defined and undefined risk strategies typically reach P/L targets at different rates and often require different management strategies.

4. The percentage of capital allocated to a single position can be calculated from the POP of the strategy and the correlation between existing portfolio positions. The percentage of portfolio capital allocated to a single position can be estimated using Equation (8.1); however, this percentage can also be scaled up because the risk-free rate yields a very conservative estimate.

Chapter 9

Binary Events

To this point, this book has highlighted unpredictable implied volatility (IV) expansions and their impact on short premium portfolios. However, traders can expect a certain class of IV expansions and contractions with near certainty. These expected volatility dynamics are the result of *binary events*. A binary event is a *known* upcoming event affecting a specific asset (or group of assets) that is *anticipated* to create a large price move. Though price variance is *expected* to increase, it may or may not actually do so depending on the outcome of the binary event.[1] Some examples of binary events include company earnings reports (motivating earnings trades), new product announcements, oil market reports, elections, and Federal Reserve announcements pertaining to the broader market.

---

[1] The term binary is used to describe systems that can exist in one of two possible states (on/off, yes/no). In this context, a binary event is a type of event where price changes either remain within expectations or exceed expectations.

Because the date of the anticipated price swing is known, there is typically significant demand for contracts expiring on or after the binary event for that underlying asset. This increased demand results in an increase in the asset's IV, which usually contracts back to nonevent levels immediately after the outcome is known. This trend is shown in Figure 9.1.

The impact from a binary event volatility expansion differs from that of unexpected periods of market volatility because the options approaching binary events are priced to reflect the expectation of large moves in the underlying. However, the high credits and immediate volatility contractions that often result from binary events do not necessarily translate into higher (or even likely) profits for short premium positions. This is because the *magnitude* of the price move following the outcome of the binary event is unpredictable, and it may meet or diverge from expectations. On average, the market response to a binary event tends to be quite large, causing the short options strategies that capitalize on these conditions to be *highly* volatile and not necessarily profitable in the long run. This phenomenon also follows from the efficient market hypothesis (EMH), as the well-understood nature of binary events challenges any consistent edge for these types of strategies.

There is no strong evidence that buying or selling premium around binary events provides a consistent edge with respect to probability of profit (POP) or average profit and loss (P/L) because a lot of the IV overstatement edge is lost in the large moves following a binary event. However, binary event trades are a very time-efficient use of capital because volatility contractions happen more rapidly and predictably than in more regular market conditions. Binary event trades may also be attractive to risk-tolerant traders as a source of market engagement. During earnings season, a single week may present up to 20 high-risk/high-reward opportunities for earnings trades. Binary event trades can also be educational for new traders wanting to learn how to adjust positions in rapidly changing, high volatility conditions outside of sell-offs. These types of trades, as they take place under unique circumstances, are structured and managed differently than typical core or supplemental positions.

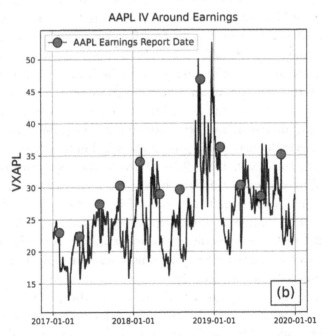

Figure 9.1 IV indexes for different stocks from 2017–2020. Assets include (a) AMZN (Amazon stock) and (b) AAPL (Apple stock).

Option Strategies for Binary Events

Because binary event trades are highly volatile and have no strong evidence of a long-term statistical edge, they should only occupy spare portfolio capital and their position size should be kept *exceptionally* small. For example, if a trader's usual position size for an AAPL strangle is a five-lot (five calls and five puts, each written for 100 shares of stock), then an AAPL earnings strangle may comprise a one- or two-lot. Additionally, underlyings for binary event trades are typically stocks, with quarterly earnings reports being the most common type of binary event. Binary event trades take place over much shorter timescales than more typical trades and must be carefully monitored. Earnings trades, for example, are typically opened the day before earnings and closed the day following earnings. This strategy limits downside risk and capitalizes on the majority of the volatility contraction, which tends to occur immediately after the binary event.

The long-term success of binary event trades is difficult to verify because there are relatively few occurrences, resulting in high statistical uncertainty. AAPL, for example, has only reported earnings roughly 100 times since the mid 1990s. The Federal Reserve holds press conferences just eight times per year, and large-scale elections take place once every two or four years. For trading strategies not built around earnings, there are thousands of data points and the statistics are more representative of long-term expectations (the central limit theorem at work). Therefore, working with this small number of data points can yield an *idea* of how binary events trades have performed in the past, but they should be taken with a large grain of salt. Tables 9.1–9.3 demonstrate how earnings trades for three different tech companies have performed over 15 years.

There is clearly significant variability in strategy performance for these three different underlyings. To reiterate, high statistical uncertainty makes it difficult to make definitive conclusions about the success of earnings trades, but some consistent trends are observable. Earnings trades are highly sensitive to changes in time. This is evidenced by the significant differences in the per-trade statistics further from the earnings announcement and demonstrates why binary event trades must be closely monitored. The *majority* of earnings trades are usually profitable, but do not necessarily average a profit in the long term because of the high per-trade standard deviation.

Table 9.1 Statistics for 45 days to expiration (DTE) 16Δ AAPL strangles from 2005–2020. Trades are opened the day before an earnings report and closed either one, five, 10, or 20 days after earnings.

AAPL Strangle Statistics (2005–2020)

Day Position Is Closed Relative to Earnings	POP	Average P/L	Standard Deviation of P/L	Conditional Value at Risk (CVaR) (5%)
Day After	72%	$85	$203	−$405
5 Days After	70%	$43	$400	−$1,027
10 Days After	61%	$60	$408	−$1,025
20 Days After	56%	−$34	$660	−$1,976

Table 9.2 Statistics for 45 DTE 16Δ AMZN strangles from 2005–2020. Trades are opened the day before an earnings report and closed either one, five, 10, or 20 days after earnings.

AMZN Strangle Statistics (2005–2020)

Day Position Is Closed Relative to Earnings	POP	Average P/L	Standard Deviation of P/L	CVaR (5%)
Day After	65%	$99	$803	−$1,927
5 Days After	65%	$85	$842	−$2,154
10 Days After	72%	$1	$1,446	−$4,416
20 Days After	76%	$78	$1,540	−$4,477

Table 9.3 Statistics for 45 DTE 16Δ GOOGL strangles from 2005–2020. Trades are opened the day before an earnings report and closed either one, five, 10, or 20 days after earnings.

GOOGL Strangle Statistics (2005–2020)

Day Position Is Closed Relative to Earnings	POP	Average P/L	Standard Deviation of P/L	CVaR (5%)
Day After	75%	−$60	$1,320	−$4,639
5 Days After	67%	−$113	$1,358	−$4,724
10 Days After	65%	−$122	$1,275	−$3,675
20 Days After	71%	−$2	$1,584	−$4,909

Per-trade variance and tail exposure also tend to increase the longer the trade is held, indicating why these types of trades should be relatively short term. This is why generally, binary event trades, such as earning trades, are closed the day following the binary event.

Takeaways

1. A binary event is a known upcoming event affecting a specific asset (or group of assets) that is anticipated to create a large price move. This anticipation creates demand for options contracts expiring on or after the binary event and an increase in the IV of the asset. IV typically contracts back to nonevent levels immediately after the outcome is known.

2. The high credits and immediate volatility contractions resulting from binary events do not necessarily translate to large or consistent short premium profits because the magnitude of the market response is unpredictable. Binary events trades are generally highly volatile and undependable sources of profit but can be used for market engagement or an educational experience for new traders.

3. Binary event trades should only occupy spare portfolio capital and their position size should be kept *exceptionally* small. Binary event trades should also take place over much shorter timescales than more typical trades, and they must be carefully monitored.

Chapter 10

Conclusion and Key Takeaways

S uccessful traders do not rely on luck. Rather, the long-term success of traders depends on their ability to obtain a consistent, statistical edge from the tools, strategies, and information available. This book introduces the core concepts of options trading and teaches new traders how to capitalize on the versatility and capital efficiency of options in a personalized and responsible way. Options are fairly complicated instruments, but this book aims to lessen the learning curve by focusing on the most essential aspects of applied options trading. The detailed framework laid out in this book can be summarized succinctly in the following key takeaways:

1. Implied volatility (IV) is a proxy for the sentiment of market risk derived from supply and demand for financial insurance. When options prices increase, IV increases; when options prices decrease, IV decreases. IV gives the perceived magnitude of future movements and is not directional. It can also be used to approximate the one

169

standard deviation expected price range of an asset (although this does not take strike skew into account). The CBOE Volatility Index (VIX) is meant to track the IV for the S&P 500 and is used as a proxy for the perceived risk of the broader market. The VIX, like all volatility signals, is assumed to revert down following significant expansions, which indicates some statistical validity in making downward directional assumptions about volatility once it is inflated.

2. Compared to long premium strategies, short premium strategies yield more consistent profits and have the long-term statistical advantage. The trade-off for receiving consistent profits is exposure to large and sometimes undefined losses, which is why the two most important goals of a short premium trader are to profit consistently enough to cover moderate, more likely losses and to construct a portfolio that can survive unlikely extreme losses.

3. The profitability of short options strategies depends on having a large number of occurrences to reach positive statistical averages, a consequence of the law of large numbers and the central limit theorem. At minimum, approximately 200 occurrences are needed for the average profit and loss (P/L) of a strategy to converge to long-term profit targets and more is better.

4. Extreme losses for short premium positions are highly unlikely but typically happen when price swings in the underlying are large while the expected move range is tight (low IV). Because large price movements in low IV are rare and difficult to reliably model, the most effective way to reduce this exposure is to trade short premium once IV is elevated.

5. Although high volatility environments are ideal for short premium positions, short premium positions have high probability of profits (POPs) and some statistical edge in all volatility environments. Additionally, because volatility is low the majority of the time, trading short options strategies in *all* IV environments allows traders to profit more consistently and increases the number of occurrences. To manage exposure to outlier risk when adopting this strategy, it is essential to maintain small position sizes and limit the amount of capital allocated to short premium positions, especially when IV is

low. This strategy can be further improved by scaling the amount of capital allocated to short premium according to the current market conditions.

VIX Range	Maximum Portfolio Allocation
0–15	25%
15–20	30%
20–30	35%
30–40	40%
40+	50%

6. Buying power reduction (BPR) is the amount of portfolio capital required to place and maintain an option trade. The BPR for long options is merely the cost of the contract, and the BPR for short options is meant to encompass at least 95% of the potential losses for exchange-traded fund (ETF) underlyings and 90% of the potential losses for stock underlyings. BPR is used to evaluate short premium risk on a trade-by-trade basis in two ways: BPR is a fairly reliable metric for the worst-case loss of an undefined risk position, and BPR is used to determine if a position is appropriate for a portfolio based on its buying power. A defined risk trade should not occupy more than 5% of portfolio buying power and an undefined risk trade should not occupy more than 7%, with exceptions allowed for small accounts. The formulae for BPR are complicated and specific to the type of strategy, but the BPR for short strangles is approximately 20% of the price of the underlying. BPR can be used to compare the risk for variations of the same strategy (e.g., strangle on underlying A versus strangle on underlying B), but it cannot be used to compare risk for strategies with different risk profiles (e.g., strangle on underlying A versus iron condor on underlying A).

7. Traders trade according to their personal profit goals, risk tolerances, and market beliefs, but it is generally good practice to be aware of the following:

   • Only trade underlyings with liquid options markets to minimize illiquidity risk.

- The choice of underlying is somewhat arbitrary, but it's important to select an underlying with an appropriate level of risk. Stock underlyings tend to be higher-risk, higher-reward than ETF underlyings. This means stock underlyings present high IV opportunities more frequently, but they have more tail loss exposure and are more expensive to trade.

- Choose a contract duration that is an efficient use of buying power, allows for consistency, offers a reasonable number of occurrences, has manageable P/L swings throughout the duration, and has moderate ending P/L variability. Durations between 30 and 60 days are suitable for most traders.

- Compared to defined risk trades, undefined risk trades have higher POPs, higher profit potentials, unlimited downside risk, and higher BPRs. High-POP defined risk trades, such as wide iron condors, have comparable risk profiles to undefined risk trades while also offering protection from extreme losses. Such trades can be better suited for low IV conditions compared to undefined risk trades and are allowed to occupy undefined risk portfolio capital.

- Contracts with higher deltas are higher-risk, higher-reward than contracts with lower deltas. When trading premium, consider contracts between 10Δ and 40Δ, which is large enough to achieve a reasonable amount of growth but small enough to have manageable P/L swings and ending P/L variability.

8. When choosing a management strategy, the primary factors to consider are convenience and consistency, capital allocation preferences, desired number of occurrences, per-trade average P/L, and per-trade exposure. Early-managed positions have lower per-trade P/Ls but less tail risk than positions held to expiration. Because managing early also accommodates more occurrences and averages more P/L per day, closing positions prior to expiration and redeploying capital to new positions is generally a more efficient use of capital compared to extracting more value from an existing position.

   - If managing according to days to expiration (DTE), consider closing trades around the contract duration midpoint to achieve a decent amount of long-term profit and justify the tail loss exposure.

- If managing an undefined position according to a profit target, choosing a target between 50% and 75% of the initial credit allows for reasonable profits while also reducing the potential magnitude of outlier losses. Choosing a profit target that is too low reduces average P/L, and choosing a profit target that is too high does little to mitigate outlier risk. Profit targets for defined risk positions can be lower because they are generally less volatile.
- If combining strategies, managing undefined risk contracts at either 50% of the initial credit or halfway through the contract duration generally achieves reasonable, consistent profits and moderates outlier risk.
- If implementing a stop loss, a mid-range stop loss threshold of at least −200% of the initial credit is practical. If the stop loss is too small (−50% for example), losses are more likely since options have significant P/L variance, although they often recover. It's also important to note that stop losses do not guarantee a maximum loss in cases of rapid price movements, so stop losses are typically paired with another management strategy unless trading passively. Stop losses are generally not suitable for defined risk strategies.

9. Maintaining the capital allocation guidelines is crucial for limiting tail exposure and achieving a reasonable amount of long-term growth:
    - The amount of portfolio buying power allotted to short premium positions, such as short strangles and short iron condors, should range from 25% to 50% depending on the current market volatility, with the remaining capital either kept in cash or a low-risk passive investment. [refer to Takeaway 5].
    - Of the amount allocated to short premium, at least 75% should be reserved for undefined risk trades (with less than 7% of portfolio buying power allocated to a single position) and at most 25% reserved for defined risk strategies (with less than 5% of portfolio buying power allocated to a single position) [refer to Takeaway 6].
    - Generally speaking, at most 25% of the capital allocated to short premium should go toward supplemental positions, or higher-risk, higher-reward trades that are tools for market engagement. The remainder should go toward core positions or trades with high POPs and moderate P/L variation that offer consistent profits and reasonable outlier exposure.

10. Diversifying the underlyings of an options portfolio (i.e., trading a collection of assets with low correlations) is one of the most essential diversification tools for portfolio risk management, particularly outlier risk management. Strategy diversification and duration diversification, though not as essential as underlying diversification, are other straightforward risk management techniques.

11. The Greeks form a set of risk measures that quantify different dimensions of exposure for options. Each contract has its own specific set of Greeks, but some Greeks are additive across positions with different underlyings. Consequently, these metrics can be used to summarize the various sources of risk for a portfolio and guide adjustments. Two key Greeks are beta-weighted delta ($\beta\Delta$) and theta (θ). Beta-weighted delta represents the amount of directional exposure a position has relative to some index rather than the underlying itself. Theta represents the expected decrease in an option's value per day. $\beta\Delta$ neutral portfolios are attractive to investors because they are relatively insensitive to directional moves in the market and profit from changes in IV and time.

12. Because short-premium traders consistently profit from time decay, the total theta across positions gives a reliable estimate for the expected daily growth of a short options portfolio. The minimum theta ratio ($\theta_{\text{portfolio}}$/net liquidity) for an options portfolio should range from 0.05% to 0.1% and should not exceed 0.2% because this indicates excessive risk. If a portfolio is not meeting these theta ratio guidelines, then the positions should be adjusted as follows:

    • If a properly allocated, well-diversified portfolio is $\beta\Delta$ neutral but does not provide a sufficient amount of theta, then the positions in the portfolio should be reevaluated. In this case, perhaps some defined risk trades should be replaced with undefined risk trades or undefined risk positions be rolled to higher deltas. New delta neutral positions can also be added, such as strangles and iron condors, for example. IV and theta are also highly correlated, meaning that higher IV underlyings could also be considered if theta is too low. These measures can be reversed if the portfolio has too much theta exposure while being $\beta\Delta$ neutral.

    • If the theta ratio is too low (<0.1%) and the portfolio is not $\beta\Delta$ neutral, then either existing positions should be re-centered or tightened or new short premium positions should be added.

- If the $\beta\Delta$ is too large and positive (bullish), then add new negative $\beta\Delta$ positions (e.g., add short calls on positive beta underlyings or add short puts on negative beta underlyings).

- If the $\beta\Delta$ is too large and negative (bearish), then add new positive $\beta\Delta$ positions (e.g., add short puts on positive beta underlyings).

- If the theta ratio is too large (>0.2%) and the portfolio is not $\beta\Delta$ neutral, then either existing positions should be re-centered or widened or short premium positions should be removed.
  - If the $\beta\Delta$ is too large and positive (bullish), then remove positive $\beta\Delta$ positions (e.g., remove short puts on positive beta underlyings).
  - If the $\beta\Delta$ is too large and negative (bearish), then remove negative $\beta\Delta$ positions (e.g., remove short calls on positive beta underlyings).

- If a properly allocated, well-diversified portfolio provides a sufficient amount of theta but is not $\beta\Delta$ neutral, then existing positions should be reevaluated. For example, skewed positions could be closed and re-centered or replaced with new delta-neutral positions that offer comparable amounts of theta.

13. Binary event trades, such as trades around quarterly earnings reports, should be traded cautiously, only occupy spare portfolio capital, and their position size should be kept exceptionally small. Binary event trades must be carefully monitored and typically take place over much shorter timescales than more typical trades. They are often opened the day before a binary event and closed the day after.

Options trading is not for everyone. However, for traders who are prepared to understand the complex risk profiles of options, comfortable accepting a certain level of exposure, and willing to commit the time to active trading, short premium strategies can offer a probabilistic edge and the potential to profit in any type of market. There is no "right" way to trade these instruments; all traders have unique profit goals and risk tolerances. It is our hope that this book will guide traders to make informed decisions that best align with their personal objectives.

Appendix

I. The Logarithm, Log-Normal Distribution, and Geometric Brownian Motion, *with contributions from Jacob Perlman*

For the following section, let S_0 be the initial value of some asset or collection of assets and S_T the value at time T. Given the goals of investing, the most obvious statistic to evaluate an investment or portfolio is the profit or loss: $S_T - S_0$. However, according to the efficient market hypothesis (EMH), assets should be judged relative to their initial size, represented using returns, $\frac{S_T}{S_0}$.

The returns of the asset from time 0 to time T can also be written in terms of each individual return over that time frame. More specifically, for an integer N, if $t_k = \frac{k}{N} \cdot T$ then the returns, $\frac{S_T}{S_0}$, can be split into a telescoping[1] product.

$$\frac{S_T}{S_0} = \frac{S_{t_1}}{S_{t_0}} \cdot \frac{S_{t_2}}{S_{t_1}} \cdot \ \dots\ \cdot \frac{S_{t_{N-1}}}{S_{t_{N-2}}} \cdot \frac{S_{t_N}}{S_{t_{N-1}}} \tag{A.1}$$

---

[1] So called because adjacent numerators and denominators cancel, allowing the long product to be collapsed like a telescope.

The EMH states that each term in this product should be independent and similarly distributed. The central limit theorem, and many other powerful tools in probability theory, concern long *sums* of independent random variables. To apply these tools to this telescoping product of random variables, it first must be converted into a sum of random variables. Logarithms offer a convenient way to accomplish this.

Logarithmic functions are a class of functions with wide applications in science and mathematics. Though there are several equivalent definitions, the simplest is as the inverse of exponentiation. If x and b are positive numbers, and $b \neq 1$, then $\log_b x$ (read as "the log base b of x") is the number such that $b^{\log_b x} = x$. For example, $4^2 = 16$ can be equivalently written as $\log_4(16) = 2$.

The choice of base is largely arbitrary, only affecting the logarithm by a constant multiple. If $c \neq 1$ is another possible base, then $\log_c x = \frac{1}{\log_b c} \log_b x$. In mathematics, the most common choice is Euler's constant, a special number: $e \approx 2.718$. Using this constant as a base results in the *natural logarithm*, denoted $\ln x = \log_e x$. The justification for this choice largely comes down to notational convenience, such as when taking derivatives: $\frac{d \log_b x}{dx} = \frac{1}{\log_e b} \frac{1}{x}$. In this example, as $\log_e e = 1$, using ln avoids the accumulation of cumbersome and not particularly meaningful constant factors.

As $e^x \cdot e^y = e^{x+y}$, logarithms have the useful property[2] given by:

$$\ln(x \cdot y) = \ln(x) + \ln(y) \tag{A.2}$$

This property transforms the telescoping product given above into a sum of small independent pieces, given by the following equation:

$$\ln \frac{S_T}{S_0} = \ln \frac{S_{t_1}}{S_{t_0}} + \ln \frac{S_{t_2}}{S_{t_1}} + \dots + \ln \frac{S_{t_{N-1}}}{S_{t_{N-2}}} + \ln \frac{S_{t_N}}{S_{t_{N-1}}} \tag{A.3}$$

The central limit theorem states that if a random variable is made by adding together many independently random pieces, then the result will be normally distributed. One can, therefore, conclude that log returns are normally distributed. Observe the following:

$$S_T = S_0 e^{\ln \frac{S_T}{S_0}} \tag{A.4}$$

---

[2] Stated abstractly, logarithms are the group homomorphisms between $(\mathbb{R}_{>0}, \cdot)$ and $(\mathbb{R}, +)$.

This suggests that stock prices follow a log-normal distribution or a distribution where the logarithm of a random variable is normally distributed. Within the context of Black-Scholes, this implies that stock log-returns evolve as Brownian motion (normally distributed), and stock prices evolve as geometric Brownian motion (log-normally distributed). The log-normal distribution is more appropriate to describe stock prices because the log-normal distribution cannot have negative values and is skewed according to the volatility of price, as shown in the comparisons in Figure A.1.

II. Expected Range, Strike Skew, and the Volatility Smile

The majority of this book refers to expected range approximated with the following equation:

$$1\sigma \text{ expected range (\$)} = \text{Stock price} \cdot \text{IV} \cdot \sqrt{\frac{\text{No. of Calendar Days}}{365}}$$

$$(\text{A.5})$$

For a stock trading at current price S_0 with volatility σ and risk-free rate r, the Black-Scholes theoretical 1σ price range at a future time t for this asset is given by the following equation:

$$1\sigma \text{ expected range (\$)} = S_0 e^{rt \pm \sigma\sqrt{t}} \qquad (\text{A.6})$$

The equation in (A.5) is a valid approximation of this formula when $rt \pm \sigma\sqrt{t}$ is small, which follows from the mathematical relation $e^x = 1 + x + O(x^2)$. Generally speaking, (A.5) is a very rough approximation for expected range, and it becomes less accurate in high volatility conditions, when $rt \pm \sigma\sqrt{t}$ is larger.

Though (A.5) still yields a reasonable, back-of-the-envelope estimate for expected range, the one standard deviation expected move range is calculated on most trading platforms according to the following:

$$1\sigma \text{ expected range (\$)} = 60\% \times \text{Price of ATM Straddle} + 30\% \times$$

$$\text{Price of Strangle 1 Strike from ATM} + 10\% \times$$

$$\text{Price of Strangle 2 Strikes from ATM} \qquad (\text{A.7})$$

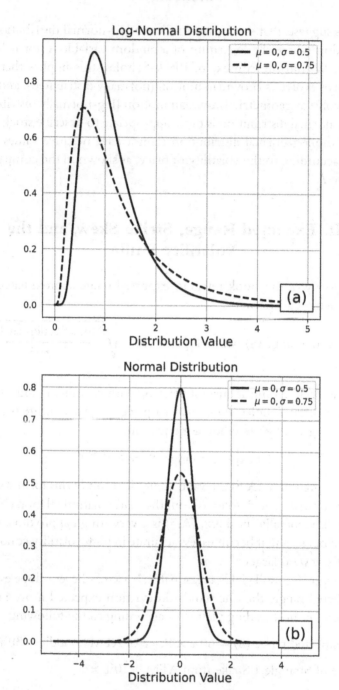

Figure A.1   Comparison of the log-normal distribution (a) and the normal distribution (b). The mean and standard deviation of the normal distribution are the exponentiated parameters of the log-normal distribution.

According to the EMH, this is simply the expected future price displacement, i.e., price of at-the-money (ATM) straddle, with additional terms (prices of near ATM strangles) to counterbalance the heavy tails pulling the expected value beyond the central 68%. To see how this formula compares with the (A.5) approximation, consider the statistics in Table A.1.

Table A.1 Expected 30-day price range approximations for an underlying with a price of $100 and implied volatility (IV) of 20%. According to the Black-Scholes model, the per-share prices for the 30-day options are $4.58 for the straddle, $3.64 for the strangle one strike from ATM, and $2.85 for the strangle two strikes from ATM.

30-Day Expected Price Range Comparison	
Equation (A.5)	Equation (A.7)
±$5.73	±$4.13

Compared to Equation (A.5), Equation (A.7) is a more attractive way to calculate expected range on trading platforms because it is computationally simpler and independent of a rigid mathematical model. However, neither of these expected range calculations take *skew* into account.

When comparing contracts across the options chain, an interesting phenomenon commonly observed is the *volatility smile*. According to the Black-Scholes model, options with the same underlying and duration should have the same implied volatility, regardless of strike price (as volatility is a property of the underlying). However, because the market values each contract differently and implied volatility is derived from from options prices, the implied volatilities across strikes often vary. A volatility smile appears when the implied volatility is lowest for contracts near ATM and increases as the strikes move further out-of-the-money (OTM). Similarly, a volatility smirk (also known as volatility skew) is a weighted volatility smile, where the options with lower strikes tend to have higher IV than options with higher strikes. The opposite of the volatility smirk is described as forward skew, which is relatively rare, having occurred, for example, with GME in early 2021. For an example of volatility skew, consider the SPY 30 days to expiration (DTE) OTM option data shown in Figure A.2.

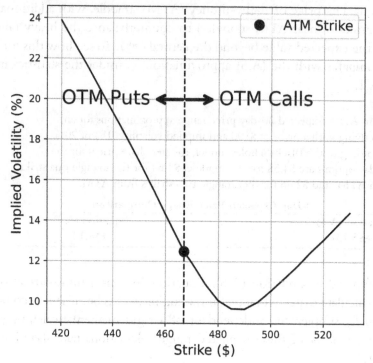

Figure A.2 Volatility curve for OTM 30 DTE SPY calls and puts, collected on November 15, 2021, after the close.

The volatility curve in Figure A.2 is clearly asymmetric around the ATM strike, with the options with lower strikes (OTM puts) having higher IVs than options with higher strikes (OTM calls). This type of curve is useful for analyzing the perceived value of OTM contracts. Compared to ATM volatility, OTM puts are generally overvalued while OTM calls are generally undervalued until very far OTM (near $510). This suggests that traders are willing to pay a higher premium to protect against downside risk compared to upside risk.

This is an example of put skew, a consequence of put contracts further from ATM being perceived as equivalently risky as call contracts closer to ATM. Table A.2 reproduces data from Chapter 5.

Table A.2 Data for 16Δ SPY strangles with different durations from April 20, 2021. The first row is the distance between the strike for a 16Δ put and the price of the underlying for different DTEs (i.e., if the price of the underlying is $100 and the strike for a 16Δ put is $95, then the put distance is [$100 – $95]/$100 = 5%). The second row is the distance between the strike for a 16Δ call and the price of the underlying for different contract durations.

16Δ SPY Option Distance from ATM

Option Type	15 DTE	30 DTE	45 DTE
Put Distance	3.9%	6.5%	8.0%
Call Distance	2.4%	3.9%	4.9%

This skew results from market fear to the *downside*, meaning the market fears larger extreme moves to the downside more than extreme moves to the upside. According to the EMH, the skew has already been priced into the current value of the underlying. Hence, the put skew implies that the market views large moves to the downside as more likely than large moves to the upside but small moves to the upside as being the most likely outcome overall. For a given duration, the strikes for the 16Δ puts and calls approximately correspond to the one standard deviation expected range of that asset over that time frame. For example, since SPY was trading at approximately $413 on April 20, 2021, the 30-day expected price move to the upside was $16 and the expected price move to the downside was $27 according to the 16Δ options.

III. Conditional Probability

Conditional probability is mentioned briefly in this book, but it is an interesting concept in probability theory worthy of a short discussion. Conditional probability is the probability that an event will occur, given that another event occurred. Consider the following examples:

- Given that the ground is wet, what is the probability that it rained?
- Given that the last roll of a fair die was six, what is the probability that the next roll will also be a six?
- Given that SPY had an up day yesterday, what is the probability it will have an up day tomorrow?

Analyzing probabilities conditionally looks at the likelihood of a given outcome within the context of known information. For events A and B the conditional probability $P(B|A)$ (read as the probability of B, given A) is calculated as follows:

$$P(B|A) = \frac{P(A \cap B)}{P(A)}$$

(A.8)

where $P(A)$ is the probability that event A occurs and $P(A \cap B)$ is the probability that A and B occur. For example, suppose A is the event that it rains on any given day and $P(A) = 0.20$ (20% chance of rain). Suppose B is the event that there is a tornado on any given day, there is a 1% chance of a tornado occurring on any given day, and tornados never happen without rain, meaning that $P(B) = P(A \cap B) = 0.01$. Therefore, given that it is a rainy day, we have the following probability that a tornado will appear:

$$\text{Probability of tornado, given rain} = P(B|A) = \frac{P(A \cap B)}{P(A)} = \frac{0.01}{0.20}$$

$$= 0.05 = 5\%$$

In other words, a tornado is five times more likely to appear if it is raining than under regular circumstances.

IV. The Kelly Criterion, *derivation courtesy of Jacob Perlman*

The Kelly Criterion is a concept from information theory and was originally created to analyze signal transmission through noisy communication channels. It can be used to determine the optimal theoretical bet size for a repeated game, presuming the odds and payouts are known. The Kelly bet size is the fraction of the bankroll that maximizes the expected long-term growth rate of the game, more specifically the logarithm of wealth. For a game with probability p of winning b and a probability $q = 1 - p$ of losing 1 (the full wager), the Kelly bet size is given as follows:

$$f = p - \frac{q}{b}$$

(A.9)

This is the theoretically optimal fraction of the bankroll to maximize the expected growth rate of the game. A brief justification for this formula follows from the paper listed in Reference 4.

- Consider a game with probability p of winning b and a probability $q = 1 - p$ of losing the full wager. If a player has W_0 in starting wealth and bets a fraction of that wealth, f, on this game, the player's goal is to choose a value of f that maximizes their wealth growth after N bets.
- If the player has N_W wins and N_L losses in the N plays of this game, then:

$$W_N = (1 + fb)^{N_W} (1 - f)^{N_L} W_0.$$

- Over many bets of this game, the log-growth rate is then given by the following:

$$\frac{1}{N} \cdot \ln\left(\frac{W_N}{W_0}\right) = \frac{N_W}{N} \ln(1 + fb) + \frac{N_L}{N} \ln(1 - f)$$

$$\rightarrow p \ln(1 + fb) + q \ln(1 - f) \text{ as } N \rightarrow \infty,$$

following from the law of large numbers
- The bet size that maximizes the long-term growth rate corresponds to $f = p - \frac{q}{b}$.

The Kelly Criterion can also be applied to asset management to determine the theoretically optimal allocation percentage for a trade with known (or approximated) probability of profit (POP) and edge. More specifically, for an option with a given duration and POP, the optimal fraction of the bankroll to allocate to this trade is approximately:

$$f = r \cdot \frac{\text{DTE}}{365} \cdot \frac{\text{POP}}{1 - \text{POP}} \tag{A.10}$$

where r is the risk-free rate and $\frac{\text{DTE}}{365}$ is the duration of the trade in years. The derivation for this equation is outlined as follows:

- For a game with probability p of winning b and a probability $q = 1 - p$ of losing 1 unit, the expected change in bankroll after one play is given by $pb - q$.

- For an investment of time t with the risk-free rate given by r, the expected change in value is estimated by $e^{rt} - 1$, derived from the future value of the game with continuous compounding. Assuming that rt is small, then $e^{rt} - 1 \approx rt$.
- For the bet to be fairly priced, the change in the bankroll should also equal rt. Therefore, if $pb - q \approx rt$, the odds for this trade can be estimated as $b \approx \frac{rt+q}{p} = \frac{1+rt}{p} - 1$.
- Using this value for b in the Kelly Criterion formula, one arrives at the following:

$$f = p - \frac{q}{b} = p - \frac{1-p}{\frac{1}{p} \cdot (1 + rt) - 1}$$

$$= \frac{(1 + rt) - p - 1 + p}{\frac{1}{p} \cdot (1 + rt) - 1} = \frac{rt}{\frac{1}{p} \cdot (1 + rt) - 1}$$

$$\approx \frac{rt}{\frac{1}{p} - 1} = rt\frac{p}{1 - p}$$

- This then yields the approximate optimal proportion of bankroll to allocate to a given trade, substituting $\frac{DTE}{365}$ for t and POP for p.

Glossary of Common Tickers, Acronyms, Variables, and Math Equations

Ticker	Full Name
SPY	SPDR S&P 500
XLE	Energy Select Sector SPDR Fund
GLD	SPDR Gold Trust
QQQ	Invesco QQQ ETF (NASDAQ-100)
TLT	iShares 20+ Year Treasury Bond ETF
SLV	iShares Silver Trust
FXE	Euro Currency ETF
XLU	Utilities ETF

Ticker	Full Name
AAPL	Apple Stock
GOOGL	Google Stock
IBM	IBM Stock
AMZN	Amazon Stock
TSLA	Tesla Stock
VIX	CBOE Volatility Index (implied volatility for the S&P 500)
GVZ	CBOE Gold Volatility Index
VXAPL	CBOE Equity VIX On Apple
VXAZN	CBOE Equity VIX On Amazon
VXN	CBOE NASDAQ-100 Volatility Index

Acronym	Full Name
NYSE	New York Stock Exchange
ETF	Exchange-Traded Fund
DTE	Days to Expiration
EMH	Efficient Market Hypothesis
ITM	In-the-Money
OTM	Out-of-the-Money
ATM	At-the-Money
P/L	Profit and Loss
IV	Implied Volatility
VaR	Value at Risk
CVaR	Conditional Value at Risk
POP	Probability of Profit
BPR	Buying Power Reduction
IVP	IV Percentile
IVR	IV Rank
NFT	Non-Fungible Tokens

Variable Symbol	Variable Name/Definition
S	Spot/stock price: the price of the underlying
V	Contract price: the price of the option, noting that C is used if the contract is a call and P is used in the case of puts
K	Strike price: the price at which the holder of an option can buy or sell an asset on or before a future date
r	Risk-free rate of return: the theoretical rate of return of a riskless asset
μ	Mean: the central tendency of a distribution
σ	Standard deviation: the spread of a distribution; also used as a measure of uncertainty or risk Volatility: the standard deviation of log-returns for an asset; a key input in options pricing
Δ	Delta: the expected change in an option's price given a \$1 increase in the price of the underlying
Γ	Gamma: the expected change in an option's delta given a \$1 change in the price of the underlying
θ	Theta: the expected time decay of an option's extrinsic value in dollars per day
β	Beta: the volatility of the stock relative to that of the overall market
$\beta\Delta$	Beta-weighted delta: the expected change in an option's price given a \$1 change in some reference index

Equation Number	Equation
1.1 Simple Returns	Simple Returns $= R_t = \dfrac{S_t - S_{t-1}}{S_{t-1}}$
1.2 Log Returns	Log Returns $= R_t = \ln\left(\dfrac{S_t}{S_{t-1}}\right)$

Equation Number	Equation
1.3 Long Call P/L	Long call P/L = $max(0, S - K) - C$
1.4 Long Put P/L	Long put P/L = $max(0, K - S) - P$
1.5 Population Mean	Mean = $\mu = \dfrac{1}{n} \cdot \sum_{i=1}^{n} x_i = \dfrac{1}{n} \cdot (x_1 + x_2 + x_3 + \cdots + x_n)$
1.6 Expected Value	$E[X] = \sum_{i=1}^{k} x_i \cdot p_i$ $= x_1 \cdot p_1 + x_2 \cdot p_2 + x_3 \cdot p_3 + \cdots + x_k \cdot p_k$
1.7 Population Variance	Variance = $\sigma^2 = \dfrac{1}{n} \cdot \sum_{i=1}^{n} (x_i - \mu)^2$
1.8 Variance	$Var(X) = E[(X - E[X])^2] = E[X^2] - E[X]^2$ $= (x_1^2 \cdot p_1 + x_2^2 \cdot p_2 + x_3^2 \cdot p_3 + \ldots + x_k^2 \cdot p_k)$ $- (x_1 \cdot p_1 + x_2 \cdot p_2 + x_3 \cdot p_3 + \ldots + x_k \cdot p_k)^2$
1.9 Skew	Skew = $\dfrac{1}{n} \cdot \dfrac{\sum_{i=1}^{n} (x_i - \mu)^3}{\sigma^3}$
1.15 Delta	$\Delta = \dfrac{\partial V}{\partial S}$
1.16 Gamma	$\Gamma = \dfrac{\partial \Delta}{\partial S} = \dfrac{\partial^2 V}{\partial S^2}$
1.17 Theta	$\theta = \dfrac{\partial V}{\partial t}$
1.18 Population Covariance	Covariance = $Cov(X, Y) = \dfrac{1}{n} \cdot \sum_{i=1}^{n} (x_i - \mu_X)(y_i - \mu_Y)$
1.19 Covariance	$Cov(X, Y) = E[(X - E[X])(Y - E[Y])]$

Equation Number	Equation
1.20 Correlation Coefficient	$\text{Correlation} = \rho_{XY} = \dfrac{\text{Cov}(X, Y)}{\sigma_X \sigma_Y}$
1.21 Additive Property of Variance	$\text{Var}(X + Y) = \text{Var}(X) + \text{Var}(Y) + 2\text{Cov}(X, Y)$
1.22 Beta	$\beta = \dfrac{\text{Cov}(R_i, R_m)}{\text{Var}(R_m)}$
2.1 $\pm 1\sigma$ Expected Range Approximation (%)	$1\sigma \text{ expected range } (\%) =$ $\text{IV} \cdot \sqrt{\dfrac{\text{No. of Calendar Days}}{365}}$
2.2 $\pm 1\sigma$ Expected Range Approximation ($)	$1\sigma \text{ expected range } (\$) =$ $\text{Stock price} \cdot \text{IV} \cdot \sqrt{\dfrac{\text{No. of Calendar Days}}{365}}$
3.1 IV Percentile (IVP)	$\text{IVP} = \dfrac{\text{Number of trading days in past year with IV below current IV}}{252}$
3.2 IV Rank (IVR)	$\text{IVR} = \dfrac{\text{Current IV} - \text{Min. IV over past year}}{\text{Max. IV over past year} - \text{Min. IV over past year}}$
4.1 Short Put BPR	**Short Put BPR** $= max(((0.2 \times S) - (S - K)) \times 100, (0.1 \times K) \times 100, 250 - P \times 100)$
4.2 Short Call BPR	**Short Call BPR** $= max(((0.2 \times S) - (K - S)) \times 100, (0.1 \times K) \times 100, 250 - C \times 100)$

Equation Number	Equation
4.3 Short Strangle BPR	Short Strangle BPR = *max*(Put BPR, Call BPR)
5.1 Short Iron Condor BPR	Short Iron Condor BPR = 100 × *max*(long call strike − short call strike, short put strike − long put strike) − 100 × (short call price + short put price − long call price − long put price)
8.1 Approximate Kelly Allocation Percentage	$f = r \cdot \dfrac{\text{DTE}}{365} \cdot \dfrac{\text{POP}}{1 - \text{POP}}$

References

1. Campbell, J. M. (1997). *The Econometrics of Financial Markets*. Princeton University Press.
2. Chriss, N. A. (1997). *Black-Scholes and Beyond: Option Pricing Models*. Irwin Professional Publishing.
3. Hull, J. C. (2015). *Options, Futures, and Other Derivatives* (9th ed.). Pearson.
4. Kelly, J. L. (1956). A new interpretation of information rate. *Bell Systems Technical Journal, 35*(4), 917–926. https://ieeexplore.ieee.org/document/6771227
5. Ross, S. M. (2005). *A First Course in Probability* (8th ed.). Pearson.
6. Shreve, S. E. (2004). *Stochastic Calculus for Finance I: The Binomial Asset Pricing Model*. Springer.

Index